DRAWING
THE NET

DRAWING
THE NET

30 Practical Principles
for Leading Others to Christ
Publicly and Personally

O. S. HAWKINS

BROADMAN
& HOLMAN
PUBLISHERS

Nashville, Tennessee

Library of Congress Cataloging-in-Publication Data

Hawkins, O. S.
   Drawing the net / O.S. Hawkins.
     p.   cm.
   ISBN 0-8054-2007-X
   1. Evangelistic invitations.   I. Title.
BV3793.H38   1993
269'.2—dc20

                                92-33580
                                    CIP

To David Hamilton

My sidekick and partner in the ministry. For almost twenty years he has been by my side as we have shared our ministries together in Oklahoma and Florida. Together we have presented the personal appeal to hundreds of people in their homes and left rejoicing.

As I have offered the public appeal thousands of times from my pulpit he has stood there "at the front" to warmly receive those who have responded, pulling for me and praying for me all the while. We share in each other's victories as though they were our own. Thanks, Dave. You are the greatest!

OTHER BOOKS BY O. S. HAWKINS

When Revival Comes
After Revival Comes
Clues to a Successful Life
Where Angels Fear to Tread
Tracing the Rainbow Through the Rain
Unmasked: Recognizing and Dealing with Imposters in the Church
Revive Us Again
Jonah: Meeting the God of the Second Chance
Getting Down to Brass Tacks: Studies in James

Table of Contents

Introduction

Introduction

"Drawing the Net" was a common phrase in the first-century Galilean world. To those who made their living as fishermen along the shores of the Sea of Galilee it meant the culmination of a fishing expedition—the harvest, if you please. Jesus spent the majority of His earthly ministry along the shores of the Sea. There He called his followers to become "fishers of men."

In fact, when it came time to choose the "team" He would use to take His message to the world, He picked some common, crusty, callous-handed fishermen for the task. He selected men who knew what it meant to become fishers of men and to draw the net. Three-and-a-half years after becoming a follower of Jesus Christ, Simon Peter, the "big fisherman," stood on the temple mount in Jerusalem, preached his monumental Pentecostal sermon, and drew the net "with many other words" (Acts 2:40). The result was 3,000 people being converted and the church being born.

When I think of "drawing the net," extending the gospel invitation, I recall "Bonefish Sam" Ellis, a fisherman par excellence. I remember the experience well. I awoke before sunrise and flicked on the hotel room light. A dozen bugs began to scamper hurriedly back into their hiding places. Stepping across the tile floor into the bathroom I managed to turn on the rusty faucet without breaking it off and produced a dribble of water for face washing and tooth brushing. There are few modern conveniences on the island of Bimini. There is only one small street that winds its way over the length of the island. The one night spot is "Papa Hemingway's" where the goombay music of the island fills the evening air. But I was not on Bimini for convenience sake. I was there to catch the elusive bonefish of the Bimini flats, pound for pound the greatest sport fish in all the world!

Bonefish Sam was there in his flat-bottom boat to pick me up right on schedule. This crusty old fishing guide is a legend in those parts, having been on the cover of *Life* magazine in years gone by and having fished with much of the royalty of the world. Sam has spent his life fishing the flats, and, though he is older now, he can still spot a three-inch dorsal fin above the water a football field away. Bonefishing is actually more hunting than fishing. It is an art within itself and "hooking" four or five and "boating" two or three make for a supremely successful day.

Sam and I fished all day under the blistering sun. I learned more about life that day from "Bonefish Sam" than I did about fishing. Late that afternoon, flying back toward the sunset to Fort Lauderdale, I jotted down a few words in my journal to describe this seasoned legend of the flats. The first word that came to my mind was *positive*. Early that morning as we boated away from the dock, his first words were, "Today is the day! There is a world-record bonefish out there just waiting for us!" By the time we made it to the flats, he had me so pumped up and excited I was already wondering whether to hang my record trophy at the office or in my home. I learned right then that a true fisherman is always positive. The big one is always only a cast away!

As I continued reminiscing over the day while looking at the azure Atlantic below, I wrote under *positive* the word *persistent*. That was Bonefish Sam personified. By noon I had been blistered by the sun, battered by the waves, and, to top it off, we had not even seen the first sight of a bonefish, much less had a nibble. I was ready to head for shore and spend the rest of the day lying leisurely under a palm tree with a good book. Not Sam! Winston Churchill undoubtedly learned his famous "Never-Give-Up" speech from Bonefish Sam Ellis. Sam kept at it through the noon hour, into the afternoon, until, yes, until we landed "the big one." Quickly the word *patient* came to mind, and I jotted it down. Sam was a true-blue fisherman and, like a real fisherman, he was patient. He never seemed to hurry, and what impressed me the most was: he was open to trying different methods. When the fish wouldn't bite a shrimp bait, he would substitute another kind. Flexibility! He was not locked into one method of fishing, and it paid off in the end.

As the small seaplane's tires screeched and bounced down the home runway, I hurriedly scribbled a final reminder of a never-to-be-forgotten man. The word? *Passionate*. We fought a large bonefish for twenty minutes until finally, when it was within ten feet of the boat (and a few hours from the taxidermist), it came out of the water, spit the hook in our direction, and off it went. Sam had a fisherman's fit. You see, a real fisherman is passionate, that is, he always hates to lose one!

I often recall Sam when I am thinking about drawing the net and recruiting men and women to be a part of "our team." I want people around me like that crusty, old callous-handed fisherman, men and women who are positive, persistent, patient, and passionate. This is the exact reason Jesus of Nazareth picked the kind of men He did to join His "team," those twelve whom He would train, motivate, and eventually send out literally to change the world. He picked the "Bonefish Sams" of His day, rough, crusty, callous-handed fishermen who had spent their lives in the fishing business. Why? Maybe because Jesus knew that a genuine fisherman is always positive, always looking for an answer in every problem instead of a problem in every answer. He also recognized that a real fisherman is persistent. He never gives up! He keeps on going. He is also patient, doesn't panic under pressure, and is willing to try different methods. And finally, Jesus was well aware that a real fisherman is passionate. He always hates to lose one.

However, unlike Bonefish Sam, Christ's followers were net fishermen. They used fishing nets approximately fifteen feet in diameter that were weighted on the edges. They were cast into the sea and then drawn back into the boat with the catch of fish. There is a sense in which these nets paint a forceful picture of the church with its call to be fishers of men. Dr. Adrian Rogers, when addressing this particular point in his classic sermon on the nets, astutely observes that a net is simply "a bunch of little nothings all tied together." What a picture of the church! This is who we are, simply a bunch of little nothings all tied together.

We read in the Scriptures on different occasions how the fishermen along the Sea of Galilee "mended" their nets. When there were tears in the cords, it would cost them in the catch. The fish would escape from the net. It is vitally important that the church is "tied together" in love and unity. If there are rips in the fellowship, it will cost us in the harvest. Many churches see few souls saved, and it is not necessarily because they are not drawing the net. The problem lies in the fact that the net is full of holes!

Another important factor in net fishing is washing the nets. The Scripture records that the disciples "washed their nets" when Jesus appeared to them. A net is designed to glide through the water without being seen. However, when it contains debris, moss, or other trash particles, it does not glide as smoothly, and scares the fish away. And, if left unclean, it will eventually rot. It is important that we, in the church (the net, if you please), are clean before God. If our life-styles are dirty it eventually costs us in the harvest. Many churches see few people saved, and it is often not because the net is not drawn. Far too often it is because those in leadership do not lead clean life-styles before God and people, and consequently, the fish are scared away.

It is not enough for the net to be mended and clean, if it is not cast! There are plenty of churches that live in unity and love and live clean life-styles yet never cast the net where the fish are to be found, that is, outside the four walls of the church. When the pastor publicly preaches the message of Christ, he is "casting the net." When the layman personally shares his or her faith, he or she is casting the net. It is impossible to be a "fisher of men" if we do not cast the net.

However, there is one other element in net fishing. And, unfortunately, it is too often neglected. Some mend their nets (live in love and unity with each other), wash their nets (live life-styles that are clean before God), and cast their nets (that is, they share their faith), and yet they fail to draw the net back into the boat.

Drawing the net is what the preacher or layman does when he extends the gospel invitation. Drawing the net is what the Christian does when, after presenting the message of salvation, he calls for a decision. Drawing the net is what Peter did at Pentecost when the Bible says, "With many other words he warned them; and he pleaded with them [to come to Christ]."

This book is designed to equip the reader to become better prepared to extend the invitation of the good news publicly as well as personally. It is for the pastor in his pulpit. It is for the businessman sitting next to a lost person on an airplane. It is for the young man sitting across the lunch table at school. It is for the lady in the courtroom or the boy on the football team. It is designed for the bivocational pastor, the evangelist who wants to sharpen his tools. In short, this volume is designed for anyone anywhere who will take serious the call of Christ and become active in . . . *drawing the net!*

Chapter 1
Make It Prophetic

Easter is always the most special and best-attended Sunday on the church calendar. This past Easter brought unparalleled crowds to our First Baptist Church. The parking lots and garages were full as people continued to come.

The busiest person of the day was the Fort Lauderdale traffic policeman standing at the major intersection as thousands of worshipers converged on the scene. With a long blast of his whistle, he would stretch forth his hand to oncoming traffic for them to stop. And they did! With another blast of his whistle, he would look in the direction of the others. With a long, arching movement of his other arm, he would command them to move through the intersection. And they did!

Now think about that. All of those hundreds of massive machines and one lone man in the middle of an intersection. Within himself he did not have the power to stop those mighty Mac trucks, powerful Porsches, and mighty Mercurys. They could have run right over him with no problem at all. But they didn't. They stopped. Why? In one word—*authority*! That policeman had all the authority of the city government of Fort Lauderdale, Florida, behind him, and when he signaled "Go," people went, and when he indicated "Stop," they did.

Where do we receive our authority when we, as God's spokesmen, stand in the intersection of life and offer Christ's appeal for men and women to receive the free gift of eternal life? What is the source of our authority when we stand behind the pulpit and appeal to our hearers to accept Christ as one's personal Savior? What authority do we have when we ask a friend across the lunch table, "Would you like to invite Christ into your heart?"

When *anyone anywhere* appeals to another to trust Christ, one does so, like God's "policeman" at an intersection, with all the authority of heaven. When we offer Christ's appeal, we should make sure it is prophetic. By that I mean authoritative and Bible-based.

When Simon Peter stood before the multitude on the Day of Pentecost he opened the scroll to Joel 2:28-32 and established a prophetic, biblical basis for: (1) what was happening and (2) what he desired his hearers to do in response. He continued to interject the Scriptures (Pss. 16; 110) throughout his message. His appeal was prophetic and biblical with the authority of heaven behind it. It is alarming and appalling today how few preachers seem to use the Word of God. To offer an appeal to receive Christ without being prophetic (biblical) would be like a surgeon going into surgery without a scalpel. The Word of God is what "cuts to the heart," as evidenced in Peter's Pentecostal proclamation.

Those who enjoy the greatest harvest in their public and personal appeals for others to follow Christ have a common characteristic. They are prophetic, in the sense that they strongly emphasize the Word of God in their approach. This is a basic clue to Billy Graham's successful public ministry, as perhaps dozens of times in any message and appeal, his voice echoes, and his proclamation is punctuated with the phrase, "The Bible says. . . ."

Being prophetic in our appeal is *profitable*. The apostle Paul wrote to his young understudy Timothy reminding him that "All Scripture is God-breathed and is useful for teaching, rebuking, correcting and training in righteousness, so that the man of God may be thoroughly equipped for every good work" (2 Tim. 3:16-17). An effective appeal is a balanced appeal. That is, it is doctrinally sound, reproves, gently corrects, and instructs in righteousness. Some see little fruit because their appeals are out of balance, and they "go to seed" on one particular element. Some appeals are full of doctrine to the exclusion of instruction. Others go overboard on rebuking and turn people away in the process. Still others think every appeal must be used to correct everyone else. Like Peter's Pentecostal invitation (Acts 2) and Paul's Pisidian entreaty (Acts 13), an effective appeal is balanced.

From Genesis to Revelation we view the illustration of this prophetic, authoritative (not authoritarian) appeal. Do you remember in Genesis 3:9 when God appealed to Adam to restore the broken fellowship? "Where are you [Adam]?" He asked. That is the question I want my hearers to confront. God knew where Adam was, but He wanted Adam to know where Adam was! From Joshua in Canaan with heaven's authority behind him, saying, "Choose for yourselves this day whom you will serve. . . . But as for me and my household, we will serve the Lord" (Josh. 24:15)— to Elijah on Mount Carmel, crying, "How long will you waver between two opinions? If the Lord is God, follow him; but if Baal is God, follow him" (1 Kings 18:21)—all the way to the last page of the Bible there is this prophetic

appeal, "The Spirit and the bride say 'Come!' . . . Whoever
is thirsty, let him come; and whoever wishes, let him take
the free gift of the water of life" (Rev. 22:17).

Appeal from cover to cover! It is our source of prophetic
authority, and when we proclaim the Word, we do so with
heaven's authority behind us. Whether we are appealing
to others publicly or privately, the appeal should be Bible-
based and we should . . . *make it prophetic!*

Chapter 2
Make It Plain

As we issue Christ's appeal, one of the most severe obstacles is the assumption that our hearers understand what we are seeking to articulate and asking them to do. Many people who are recipients of our appeals have had little or no church environment for years. Yet, we often speak to them in words and phrases we assume they understand. Every week I'm preaching to people who have not been inside a church since childhood. For many others it is the first time they have ever been in any evangelical church.

Picture in your mind that man or woman in church for the first time, and the pastor comes to the end of the sermon by announcing, "We will now turn to hymn number 240. Won't you come?" Though all the "old-timers" know what he means, the very person he is trying to reach begins to ask himself several questions. *Come to whom? Why? Come for what? When? Where?* Many of us cast the net but never draw it in because we "assume" our hearers understand what we are asking them to do. Many of them don't! So we must make it plain.

Many of the words we frequently use in our "ecclesiastical" vocabularies are like a foreign language to the men and women we are attempting to reach for Christ. For example, consider the young-adult generation is by and large without much church background or biblical training. Many do not know that Matthew, Mark, Luke, and John are books of the Bible. Some have been raised in homes where they have never heard a prayer and never seen the Bible open. This is an entire generation we are attempting to impact for Christ. Our problem is we often do not know how to think as they think because we only think as we are programmed to think. We must be as plain as we can in trying to reach a generation whose main question about us and our faith is not so much "Is it true?" but "Is it relevant?" In other words, "Does it fit?" "Is it what I need?" "Does it speak to me?" These are practical questions.

Make the appeal *plain*. When Peter gave us our pattern at Pentecost he began with, "Let me explain this to you; listen carefully to what I say" (Acts 2:14). He was being as plain as he could. He did not make it difficult. At the outset he built a bridge instead of a barrier. And the result? When he drew the net a short time later, 3,000 men and women were caught up in the appeal. Why? Because he made it plain.

I often seek mentally to transfer myself from the pulpit into the pew where sit those to whom I am appealing. I want those hearers to know exactly what I am asking them to do, to know why I am asking them to do it, to know how I am asking them to respond, and to know what they can expect to happen when they do. No surprises!

I try to make the appeal as plain as possible and assume nothing. At the end of the sermon when I extend the public appeal I spell it out. It requires an additional four to six minutes, but no one leaves wondering what they should or could have done to act on what they had heard that day. I let them know that at an appointed time, when people are seated and praying, I will ask them to leave their seats, step into the aisle, and make their way to the front.

I spend considerable time differentiating between the types of decisions that can be made. I also explain that once we have gathered, standing with heads bowed in front of the pulpit, I will lead in a prayer. I make them aware that by coming they will be saying, "I am going Christ's way today." I assure them they don't have to worry about what to say when they reach the front, that in the act of coming they will be testifying, "I want to become a follower of Christ today."

I further explain that after my prayer I will ask them to turn to their left and follow one of our church workers into the "welcome center." There, I let them know, we have some Bible study material to give them, and if they are coming as an inquirer, we will personally lead them to faith in Christ. (See appendix A.) Our welcome center is essentially our "counseling room" where a trained counselor meets personally with each individual who responds to the public appeal. Here the gospel is shared on a one-on-one basis with everyone who responds to the appeal.

Again, words are important. We are careful not to use the words "counseling room." Can you imagine what goes through the mind of a person under conviction, about to respond, when he hears a statement like this, "We are going to ask you to sit down with a counselor in the counseling room." *Not me*, he thinks, *I don't need a shrink. I'm not going to tell my deepest secrets to anyone I don't even know.* Ever so subtly that can build a barrier instead of a bridge—and often the hearer simply does nothing about it.

Whether the appeal to receive the gift of eternal life is given publicly or privately, spell it out so there are bridges in the appeal and not barriers. Leave no surprises. Above all . . . *make it plain!*

Chapter 3
Make It Positive

When the business world plays a word-association game and reaches *positive* a ready response could be *Zig Ziglar!* Zig, one of America's best-selling authors and foremost motivators, is a committed follower of the Lord Jesus Christ. I might add, he is one of my golfing buddies.

While he was speaking in Fort Lauderdale a few years ago, we played a round of golf with Tommy John and another New York Yankee pitcher, Dana Ridenour. We stepped to the first tee, and each of the ball players blasted the ball about 240 yards down the fairway. Zig teed up and hit a decent shot about 210 yards down the middle. He turned to us and remarked, "I'll never hit one like that the rest of the day!"

When we were in the golf cart and headed down the fairway, I said, "Zig, these guys have read your books, heard your tapes, and they are fighting for jobs in the starting rotation. You are Mr. Positive, and we've hardly left the first tee until you've made a negative statement." He smiled. Zig was about to teach me a lesson, and I saw it coming. "That was no negative statement," he fired back. "You've played with me before, and you know I can't hit a ball that well." He then explained the difference between positive thinking and positive believing. Positive thinking is simply a pumped-up mental attitude. Positive believing is based on fact. Zig continued, "I know the parameters of my golf game. That wasn't a negative statement. It was a statement based on fact. It was positive believing!"

When we speak of making the appeal positive we are not referring to some hyped-up, pumped-up mental attitude but rather positive believing built on and based on the promises found in God's Word. There we discover our positive note in making the appeal.

Be positive in your appeal whether publicly or privately. Many never respond to public appeals because those appeals are so void of optimism and expectancy. In place of publicly saying, "If you will come you can find a new life," or "Will you come?" begin to extend the appeal more positively. I generally say something like, "I believe many are going to come to receive the gift of eternal life and find a new beginning, and you are going to join them. You have thought about it, prayed about, even planned on it, and the only thing left—in the words of a popular athletic-shoe advertisement—is to . . . *just do it!* You will be first. Don't wait on anyone else. It is the right thing to do." Expectancy and optimism become atmospheric and contagious!

One main reason so many see so little fruit is: they do not expect anything to happen. Many of us are too timid at the "net-drawing" time because of a fear of failure. So, we fall into the manipulation mode, or we merely scold our hearers, berate them, or seek to bully them. Productive appeals are positive appeals exuding from a countenance of optimism and expectancy. It literally becomes atmospheric.

The point? When we issue Christ's appeal, whether publicly from a pulpit or privately in a parlor, we should extend it with confidence, expectancy, and optimism. We should . . . *make it positive!*

Chapter 4
Make It Personal

Making a conscious decision to become a follower of the Lord Jesus Christ is one of the most personal of life's decisions. The one making the appeal, whether publicly or privately, must be sensitive to the need of identifying on a personal level.

The types of pronouns we use in making our appeal reveal much about what we really think of ourselves in relationship to our hearers. For example, ministers with a sense of strong identity and compassion for their people frequently speak in terms of "we" and "us." Though the most aloof are often prone to speak more in terms of "they" or "them," those with exalted opinions of themselves too frequently punctuate their appeals with the perpendicular pronoun along with "me" and "mine." Think about your own use of personal pronouns.

Preaching today is mostly in the first-person plural or the third-person plural. That is, we use plenty of "we" and "they" in our public proclamations, but this kind of preaching seldom produces conviction. First- and third-person preaching is good, but there comes the time when we need to make an application and "draw the net." This is the critical moment when the one making the appeal moves from first and third person to second person—from "we" and "they" to "you"! And, not second-person plural, but second-person singular. You—*singular*. Here is the moment of challenge, the hinge of the entire gospel appeal. Many today settle into the comfort of first- and third-person appeals because of a fear of offending certain deacons, elders, large givers, civic leaders, politicians, or other hearers. It is no wonder many churches have such little power today. Our appeal should be *personal*.

An analysis of the first recorded appeal of Simon Peter (Acts 2), and the first recorded appeal of the apostle Paul (Acts 13) reveals an interesting insight. When it was time to "draw the net" they moved from first- and third-person pronouns to second-person pronouns at the critical point of the appeal. Consider Simon Peter standing on the temple mount in Jerusalem. Hear him appeal, "This man was handed over to *you* by God's set purpose and foreknowledge; and *you*, with the help of wicked men, put him to death by nailing him to the cross" (Acts 2:23, author's italics). Hear the great apostle Paul speaking in the synagogue at Antioch: "Therefore, my brothers, I want *you* to know that through Jesus Christ the forgiveness of sins is proclaimed to *you*" (13:38, author's italics).

Our proclamation of the good news must have a personal appeal. Like Peter and Paul, we should not merely aim at the head but also at the heart. This type of appeal convicts the hearts of hearers. After Peter finished his appeal the Bible reports, "When the people heard this, they were cut to the heart" (2:37).

When we are inviting persons to become followers of Christ, we are asking them to make the most personal decision they will make in their entire lifetime. For the past twenty years Lee Horne has been my life-insurance agent. When Lee sits in my home and makes his appeal to me and my future needs, he does not speak to me in terms of what "they" should do or what "we" should do. He makes his presentation and then he lays it on the line, "Now, here is what *you* should do to secure your family's future." Successful salesmen of any kind deal in second-person pronouns. And so should those of us who appeal to others to receive the gift of eternal-life insurance. By all means, whether we extend the appeal publicly or privately, we should . . . *make it personal!*

Chapter 5
Make It Penetrating

As cited in the preceding chapters, Peter's Pentecostal appeal resulted in his hearers' hearts being "cut" (Acts 2:37). The next phrase indicates that they asked, "What shall we do?" What happened when Peter issued this prophetic, plain, positive, personal appeal? It had a penetrating effect. Their hearts were "cut."

We have a word for that in our Christian vocabulary. We call it *conviction*. Many modern appeals are superficial or designed to make our hearers feel good. Some churches even exult in the fact that people can attend their services without being made to feel guilty about their life-style, whatever it may be. Simon Peter's appeal did not have that effect. It cut and pierced his hearers to the heart. Perhaps that is the reason 3,000 were saved and baptized that day, but also the reason one out of four churches in today's greatest missionary-sending denomination cannot even baptize one new convert in an entire year!

Until a person recognizes there is no hope within himself to satisfy the righteous demands of God's law, the cross is simply a farce to him. Yet, when our hearts are cut, when conviction of sin becomes a personal matter, we become aware that our only hope of being right with God is through the cross of Christ. Many people in many church services have never felt conviction. Why? Because in many cases they have never heard appeals that were prophetic, plain, positive, and personal.

Personally, I am contemporary in my approach to church growth. However, I want my hearers to grasp what Peter's hearers realized. That is, that one must take personal responsibility for the death of Jesus Christ. He died in our place! When the men and women at Pentecost realized what they had done in crucifying the Lord, their hearts were broken (vv. 23-37). In attempting to draw the net today, too few of us attempt to lead our hearers to assume personal responsibility for their sins. Consequently, many appeals are not penetrating and are left without conviction, resulting in few conversions.

Conviction always precedes conversion. The process is referred to as spiritual birth (see John 3:1-10; Titus 3:5; 1 Pet. 1:23). It is appropriately illustrated in physical birth. There must be birth pains before the child is born, and so it is with spiritual birth. We can no more experience the supernatural new birth without godly sorrow over sin, than we can experience natural physical birth without experiencing labor pains. Conviction precedes conversion. Many empty churches have computer rolls of inactive members, who merely "made a decision" early in life, knowing nothing of conviction.

My first pastorate was in the wheat-farming community of Hobart, Oklahoma. I learned much from those good, godly farmers. Being a city boy I was fascinated by farm life. I learned several things were necessary in order to grow a bountiful crop. First, the ground had to be broken. Those farmers would mount their tractors and plow their fields, breaking and busting up the sod. Then the seed was planted. Next, the wheat was cultivated, watered, and nurtured. Finally, around the first of June every year the harvest was gathered.

Many of us who make appeals for Christ wonder why we seldom experience a harvest. Could it be the ground has not been broken? The Word of God, like a sharp, two-edged sword, is the only tool that can cut to the heart. Our appeals need to penetrate, to break the ground of the heart. It doesn't matter how much seed is sown, or how much time is spent in cultivation—if the ground is not broken there will be no harvest.

When we issue Christ's appeal, publicly or privately, one of the most important things we can do is . . . *make it penetrating!*

Chapter 6
Make It Persuasive

As we seek to put heaven in touch with the human heart we should be as persuasive as possible. Again we note Peter's Pentecostal appeal as a classic example of persuading one's hearers to become followers of the Lord Jesus. When the people heard his appeal and fell under conviction (their hearts were "cut") they asked, "What shall we do?" (Acts 2:37).

God-anointed appeals, whether public or private, are persuasive. They go straight to the heart and lead people to ask, "What shall I do?" This is a vital question for anyone considering Christ's appeal. One who is under conviction of sin does not know what to do. It is not in the heart of the natural man (see 1 Cor. 2:14). We should be so persuasive in our approach that our hearers begin to wonder what they can do about the sense of profound need they are feeling.

Many appeals today fall on deaf ears, and it is not always the hearer's fault. Many appeals are not persuasive because, in place of being plain they are complicated. In place of being positive they are critical. In place of being personal they are courteous in the sense of not offending, and in place of being penetrating they are cosmetic. It is no wonder modern appeals are not leading more men and women to ask, "What shall we do?"

What persuades some to follow Christ doesn't persuade others. Take our Lord's first five followers, for example. As we are, they were different in many ways, and what appealed to some didn't to others. John, for example, was devoted and affectionate—the one whom "Jesus loved." He was the only apostle at the cross. Andrew was humble and practical. Upon finding the Lord his first impulse was to tell his brother. Peter, on the other hand, was impulsive. He wrote the book on "Type-A" personalities. Philip was skeptical and somewhat materialistic. He often had a cash register for a mind. Upon seeing the masses needing to be fed on the Galilean mountain, Philip brought up how much it would cost to feed them. And Nathanael was more meditative. He was "without guile" (see John 1:47, KJV) and content to be in the background. John and Andrew were persuaded to follow Christ through *pulpit proclamation*. They were a part of John the Baptist's congregation and joined the throngs of people who flocked to the Jordan Valley to hear him preach.

John the Baptist's appeal was not directed to social needs only, liberal or conservative causes, or universal philosophies. His appeal pointed his hearers to Jesus Christ. He sought to persuade his hearers to "[behold], the Lamb of God, who takes away the sin of the world" (v. 29). And, upon hearing this public proclamation, John and Andrew "followed Jesus" (v. 37). The pulpit can still be powerful today. It is still a means of persuading many to follow after Christ.

Simon Peter and Nathanael, on the other hand, were persuaded to follow the Lord through *personal confronta-*

tion—Peter through his family and Nathanael through his friend. Having found Christ through pulpit proclamation, Andrew's first impulse was to make an appeal to his own brother, Peter, through personal confrontation. He sought him. Then he taught him. He was persuasive. Finally, he brought him to Jesus (vv. 41-42). Philip did the same. However, his appeal was directed at a friend instead of family. He went to Nathanael, pressed the claims of Christ to his heart, and then simply and persuasively asked, "Come and see" (vv. 45-51).

We will never draw the net and win our world through pulpit proclamation only. The church needs an army of men and women who will persuasively appeal to others through personal confrontation. Andrew found Peter. Jesus found Philip. Philip found Nathanael.

Bill recently found Ralph. Kathy found Sandy. Thus the church has continued to grow through the centuries by appealing to others through personal confrontation with the gospel. The most far-reaching results were achieved in that first generation, without the use of television, radio, cassette tapes, printed material, telephones, fax machines, computers, air travel, or stadium crusades. The good news spread from lip to lip until it reached all the way to Rome itself. Within one century this one-on-one, persuasive, personal confrontation shook paganism to its center, and it all began when "[Andrew] first findeth his own brother Simon. . . . And he brought him to Jesus." (vv. 41-42, KJV).

Although they were all persuaded in different ways these first five followers of Christ were brought to essentially the same question—"What shall we do?" The Baptizer's pulpit proclamation persuaded John and Andrew, but Peter and Nathanael were persuaded by Andrew and Philip's personal confrontation. Whether we are making Christ's appeal publicly from the pulpit or personally from the parlor we should be persuasive, whether standing to the side of our pulpit or sitting on the edge of our seat.

It is amazing what personal confrontation with the gospel on Monday through Saturday will do for public proclamation of the gospel on Sunday. One of the reasons public proclamation is without much expectancy in many places is because it is void of the persuasiveness that results from personal confrontation with others of the good news.

What shall we do? That is a good question for the church to ask as we approach and enter a new century. If we were as persuasive as those at Pentecost, our people, like theirs, would be asking, "What does this mean?" (Acts 2:12). Then they would be asking, "What shall we do?" (v. 37). When we make our appeal to others to follow the Lord Jesus we should always . . . *make it persuasive!*

Chapter 7
Make It Pointed

As we make our appeals to others, it is imperative that we be pointed in telling them what we are encouraging them to do—that is, "What is the gospel?" Many see little lasting fruit because their appeal is not pointed toward calling on people to follow Christ according to the New Testament pattern. When Peter's hearers at Pentecost asked, "What shall we do?" his one-word reply was pointed, "Repent!" (Acts 2:38). He was not vague. There were no multiple-choice options. Productive appeals are pointed.

Repentance is a forgotten word in our Christian vocabulary today, primarily because many of us are confused about what it really is and how we go about it. We often confuse repentance in our appeals with *remorse*, but merely being sorry for our sin is not repentance. The rich young ruler went away "sorrowful" (Matt. 19:22, KJV) but he did not accept Christ's appeal. We also confuse repentance with *regret*, but simply wishing something had not happened is not repentance. Pilate washed his hands in regret over his deed, but he rejected Jesus Christ. Still others of us confuse repentance with *resolve*. Just being determined to take on a new set of moral standards and "turn over a new leaf" is not repentance.

What is repentance? Until this question is properly confronted our appeal will never be properly pointed. Repentance stems from a Greek word (*metanoeo*) which means "a change of mind." When one repents one basically changes one's mind about four things.

First, repentance is a change of mind about our *self*. When one genuinely repents there ensues a new attitude about one's sense of self-importance. Repentance is also a change of mind about our *sin*. We no longer see our sin as a little vice to laugh off, excuse, or minimize. We sense our sin as being so serious it put our Lord on the cross. Repentance is also a change of mind about our *Savior*. We no longer feature Him as only a great teacher or leader but as the promised Messiah, God Himself who came to save us. Finally, repentance causes us to change our mind about *salvation*. We no longer look on it as an award that can be earned or deserved, but as God's gracious gift to all who will receive it.

As a word of personal testimony, I came to know the Lord as my personal Savior at age seventeen. However, I had been following Christ and growing explosively in Him for six months before I ever actually remember hearing the word, *repentance*. But I know I repented. How? I began to love what I used to hate and hate what I used to love. Quite frankly, in my own personal appeals to others I seldom use the word, *repentance*, but I make sure I am pointed in letting my hearers know that following Christ calls for us to change our minds about ourselves, our sin, the Savior, and salvation. I also make sure I call on people to repent in a positive manner. It should not be a "turn-or-burn" approach. I personally like the pointed approach

Paul used in Romans when he wrote that it is "God's kindness that leads you toward repentance" (2:4). The word picture is of a gentle father who takes his child by the hand and leads him.

This pointed approach to the appeal is followed by every New Testament preacher. Consider John the Baptist. He appealed to his hearers to "Repent, for the kingdom of heaven is near" (Matt. 3:2). He spoke without fear or favor. Thousands came to hear him. This pointed approach was also characteristic of the Lord Jesus Himself. He commenced His ministry with the appeal to repent. The Bible says, "From that time on Jesus began to preach, 'Repent for the kingdom of heaven is near'" (4:17). He continued his ministry with the same pointed appeal. He said, "Unless you repent, you too will all perish" (Luke 13:3). Jesus not only began and continued His preaching ministry with the message of repentance, He concluded it in the same manner. Just before His ascension He reminded us all that "repentance and forgiveness of sins will be preached in his name to all nations" (Luke 24:46-47). This pointed appeal continued to be the message of all the apostles. "They went out and preached that people should repent" (Mark 6:12). It was the message of Peter. It was the message of Paul. And it should be the message of anyone anywhere who calls on others to become followers of the Lord Jesus!

General appeals call for no decisive action. Many people, particularly after public appeals, have no clue about what the speaker has challenged them to do. When we present the gospel to men and women, publicly or privately, we are confronting them with a decision, a choice. We are calling on them to change their mind and receive from God the grace gift of salvation. This demands a pointed approach. We desire our hearers to embrace the gospel. At this point it would be advisable to ask ourselves another question—*What is the gospel?* In days of confusion over the basic tenets of our faith this is where we absolutely must be pointed and plain.

I graduated from seminary and began pastoring in the 1970s. If you had told me then I would live to pastor when knowledgeable and educated pastor-teachers would be arguing for the reality of a salvation which was devoid of any repentance and discipleship, much less any evidence that one has passed from "death into life," I would never have believed it! And yet this seems to be the appeal of certain preachers today.

Over one hundred years ago Charles Haddon Spurgeon of England wrote, "I cannot conceive it possible for anyone truly to receive Christ as Savior and yet not to receive Him as Lord. A man who is really saved by grace does not need to be told that he is under solemn obligations to serve Christ. The new life within him tells him that." This is the good news. The most pointed question in all the Bible was asked by the jailer in Philippi. Having come under the conviction of the Holy Spirit, he asked Paul and Silas, "Sirs, what must I do to be saved?" And the pointed reply? "Believe on the Lord Jesus, and you will be saved" (Acts 16:30-31).

We often hear a person remark that we must "make" Jesus Lord. Nonsense. Jesus *is* Lord, and anyone who comes to Him does as such in true repentance and faith. Repentance and faith are two sides of the same coin, and they are both the gifts of God's grace and "not of works." The Bible declares that God "grants unto us repentance and faith." This should be our pointed appeal. We are partners with God in appealing to others to receive God's wonderful gift, but

we must always remember it is God alone who convicts of
sin, draws the sinner to Himself, and grants the gift of
repentance and faith. It is our responsibility to make clear
to our hearers: they are coming to Christ and not to "the
front of the church."

One reason there is such little response is because the
appeal may be so general it calls for no change of mind
that results in a change of life. Some are appealing to men
and women to change their minds, not necessarily their
lives, in the sense that the Christian life is not a changed
life—that is, we do not just decide within ourselves to take
on a new set of moral standards. It is an exchanged life. At
the moment of salvation we give God our old life, and He
puts it away, giving us one that is brand-new, so we might
walk in "newness of life" (see Rom. 6:4). A genuine
change of mind will result in a change of our life-style. The
gospel presentation will lead people down the same path
it did at Pentecost. It will cause them to ask within their
own hearts, *What must I do?* Thus, as we extend Christ's
appeal to others, whether we do so publicly or privately, it
is imperative that we . . . *make it pointed!*

Chapter 8
Make It Pious

Extending Christ's appeal calls on us to be cautious as we remember that salvation is the work of God from start to finish. "Salvation is of the Lord" (Jon. 2:9). Only the Holy Spirit can convince us of our deep need to "change our minds" and receive Christ. The Holy Spirit can be grieved and quenched by those who seek to berate, manipulate, maneuver, scold, or cajole people into a "decision." When we write of offering the appeal piously, we are not referring to "pious" in the sense of its modern connotation. We mean pious in the sense that we "fear" the Lord (live in reverential awe of Him), recognize His sovereignty, and totally depend on Him to do His work of conviction and conversion. He is the One who "adds to the church." He has not called us to be responsible for the results but to be consistent and faithful in our witness by life and lip.

There are two calls made to a person's heart. There is an outward call and an inward call. Simon Peter at Pentecost was keenly aware of this fact. He gave the outward call, but, even though all his hearers heard his outward call, not everyone was saved that day. In fact, some "mocked" him. The three thousand converted to Christ were those who heard not only the outward call but also an inward call. The ones genuinely saved that day, as in our day, were those "whom the Lord our God will call" (Acts 2:39). This is where piety is imperative in the appeal. Wherever we are, it is our assignment to extend the outward call and trust in the Holy Spirit to issue the inward call.

How can two people sit in the same pew in the same worship service, sing the same songs, hear the same sermon, in the same anointing, and their responses be in diametrical opposition to each other? One of those persons walks out of the service with no inclination to respond and sees absolutely no need to accept Christ. In contrast, the other sitting on the same pew falls under conviction of sin and openly, and often tearfully, responds to the gospel appeal. How does this happen? They both heard the outward call, but only one has sensed the inward call. At this very point, as Paul was extending the appeal by the riverside in Philippi, the Bible records, "One of those listening was a woman named Lydia, a dealer in purple cloth from the city of Thyatira, who was a worshiper of God. *The Lord opened her heart* to respond to Paul's message" (Acts 16:14, author's italics). Paul issued the outward call, and the Lord spoke to Lydia's heart, issuing the inward call.

There are a few extremists who have carried the issue of the inward call to the point of so perverting the Scriptures that they deny the free offer of good news. The fact that we should be pious in our approach, by acknowledging that salvation is God's work, should not diminish our intensity in issuing the appeal and sharing the glorious gospel with every last person on the planet. In fact, the awareness that we are participating with the Father, Himself, in this miraculous work of salvation should give us added confidence and new boldness.

It is our purpose to extend the outward call and trust Him to do the work of issuing the inward call by opening our hearers' hearts. What a privilege is ours to be Christ's extended hand, whether we stand behind a pulpit, sit in a locker room, visit around the coffee table, or sit on a seat next to someone on an airplane. Jesus said, "As the Father has sent me, I am sending you" (John 20:21). And let's not forget why the Father "sent" the Lord Jesus to earth. "The Son of Man came to seek and to save what was lost" (Luke 19:10). We cannot save men and women, but we can seek them. We can extend the outward call and leave the results to Him, for only the Holy Spirit can offer the inward call.

Perhaps the point is best made in the words of an old hymn: "All is vain unless the Spirit/Of the Holy One comes down." Be sensitive as you extend the appeal. You are in partnership with God. Don't try to do the work of the Holy Spirit. We can trust Him. He is often grieved and quenched by our manipulation and man-centered methods. The last invitation of the Bible beckons, "The Spirit and the bride say, 'Come!'... Whoever is thirsty, let him come; and whoever wishes, let him take the free gift of the water of life" (Rev. 22:17).

There we see it plainly, left for all posterity on the last page of the Bible! The bride (the church of the Lord Jesus Christ) calls, "Come!" This is the outward call. But that is not all. The Spirit summons, "Come!" This is the inward call. And both are essential and pivotal in "drawing the net" and reaching our world for Christ. The next time you extend Christ's appeal publicly or privately... *make it pious.*

Chapter 9
Make It Pressing

If, indeed, the privilege of drawing the net is the most valuable work in the world, it should be done with persistence and a sense of urgency. It should be pressing.

After Peter finished his message at Pentecost, the Bible records that "with many other words; . . . he pleaded with them" (Acts 2:40). Yes, he was pressing for a decision from his hearers. The word we translate into our English Bibles as *plead* is derived from a Greek verb which means "to beseech with strong force" or "to call forth." It is a calling to one's side.

The word describes what happened at the Alamo in Texas in 1836. The Texans holed up in the Alamo were facing certain death and were trying to "buy time" for Sam Houston's forces to assemble near what is now Houston. Santa Anna's Mexican army was only twenty-four hours away from laying seige to the Alamo. Colonel Travis gathered his men in the courtyard on that fateful night. With his sword he drew a line in the sand and challenged those who would stay with him and fight for the cause to cross over the line. The rest is history. It was a calling to one's side. All this is wrapped up in the model appeal of Peter as he urgently and persistently besought his hearers—with strong force—to come to Christ's side.

In the Pentecostal appeal Peter did not just issue the call, sit down, and look humble. He didn't finish his sermon and suggest, "Now, let's sing a hymn. If by chance there is anyone here who would like to stand for Christ you may do so at this time. But please do not feel like you have to." Neither did he invite, "Now, if you want to make a decision, you may meet with the elders of the church," or, "You may meet with our membership committee next month." No! Peter did not apologize. As he finished his sermon he then pled for souls and pressed for decisions in the power of God the Holy Spirit. Surely there was pathos in his voice and urgency on his countenance.

Those who extended the appeal in the Bible made it pressing. Paul pressed the claims of Christ to King Agrippa's heart, and the Bible records he almost persuaded him (see Acts 26:28). One of our deepest needs, as we seek to draw the net, is to recapture this spirit of urgency and press for decisions in the power of God's Spirit.

Perhaps we should put it in a more-modern vernacular and "ask for the sale." It is amazing how few people actually "cross this line" in the gospel presentation and appeal. Many move right up to it, but few actually cross it by asking a person, "Would you like to receive Jesus Christ as your Savior right now?"

Can you imagine an attorney not asking the jury in his closing argument to decide in favor of his client? Look at him. He has spent weeks and maybe months preparing his case. He has presented his case to the jury in his opening arguments; he has used witnesses to attest to the truth of his client; he has answered every objection raised;

he has introduced indisputable evidence and facts into the case; and he has given a convincing closing argument. But suddenly he closes his briefcase and leaves the courtroom before the trial has concluded, without finishing his final argument with an appeal to the jury to "cross the line" and decide the case in favor of his client. Surely that is not going to happen with a sane lawyer! And yet, it happens so often with those of us who are advocating the gospel of Jesus Christ. We present our case, even call our witnesses, and then close our briefcase (Bible), and walk away when it comes time to press for the decision.

As a teenager I had a job after school and on Saturdays at a local shoe store. My boss, Richard Rice, taught me plenty about selling shoes in those formative years that has spilled over into other areas of life. Among many lessons, he taught me a work ethic and how to be winsome and persuasive with the customers. Most of all, he taught me how to "ask for the sale."

He assured me we had a good, quality product that would make for a satisfied customer, reminding me the customer had a desire for our product or he would not have come to us. Both the need and the want were there. My job was to meet that need with the proper fit and the right size, and then, in those often-repeated words of Mr. Rice, *ask for the sale!*

Once the customer had taken a few steps and looked admiringly in the floor mirror, I would often ask, "Would you like to wear them or would you like me to put them in a box for you?" Mr. Rice taught me to ask for the sale, and I have often thought of him down through the years when I have led someone to faith in Christ after asking, "Would you like to receive the free gift of eternal life *right now*?" He taught me a strategic principle: *ask for the sale!*

We who have experienced the joy of knowing Jesus Christ personally and enjoy the assurance of having eternal life also possess the responsibility of sharing Him with others. We who have received His power are to be His witnesses to a world in spiritual darkness. Quite frankly, it is not enough to be plain and personal, positive and persuasive, or even pointed and pious. We must "ask for the sale." Whether you are called on to offer Christ's appeal publicly in the pulpit or, personally 30,000 feet above the earth on a plane, sense the urgency of the moment. Cross over the line. Ask for the sale. In short . . . *make it pressing!*

Chapter 10
Make It Passionate

In the preceding chapter I emphasized the necessity of making the appeal pressing. Now we focus on the value of issuing it from a passionate heart.

If we press for decisions with fleshly means and motives, such will result, in the long run, as nothing but a "sounding brass and tinkling cymbal." Yet, when the appeal is pressed out of the passion of a heart burning for God, it will produce lasting results. I sometimes fear we attempt to become too "professional" in our approach. Our generation's ministry is blessed with all the modern technology of computer science at our fingertips, Christian book stores in many communities, audio and video-tape helps, seminars and conferences by the hundreds, and around-the-clock Christian television and radio. The danger today is in being prone to substitute these for the passion that comes only from being alone with God and His Word and personally sharing our faith with others.

Where do we acquire the passion needed in our public appeals? One with discernment can listen to a person issue a public appeal and usually tell in an instant whether that person is a soul-winner. It normally shows in the passion of his voice and countenance. If the preacher is not issuing the appeal personally day by day, it is difficult productively to issue the appeal in the pulpit.

There is an untrue ring about it. It is void of fervor. It is sheer hypocrisy to offer the public invitation when one seldom or never invites men and women to receive Christ privately in the normal traffic patterns of life. The heart of our greatest need is for all Christ's followers to be active in sharing their faith personally, especially those of us who are called vocationally into the gospel ministry. The Southern Baptist Convention with around 39,000 churches and fifteen million members is the greatest missionary-sending denomination in church history. Yet, annually in the United States one-fourth of the churches cannot win to Christ and baptize a single convert. In fifty-two weeks of public appeals ten thousand pastors cannot reproduce themselves, much less train their members to do so. Why? There is often little passion in the pulpit. Real passion issues from a life-style that shares Christ personally with others and presses for a decision in the power of the Holy Spirit—with a burning heart spilling over onto others around us. Passion in public proclamation issues from passion in personal and private proclamation in the home, the office, an airplane, or the social arena.

My mentor in the ministry was W. Fred Swank, for forty-three years pastor of the Sagamore Hill Baptist Church in Fort Worth, Texas. His preaching and passionate appeal led me to Christ. He baptized me, was instrumental in my "call to preach," officiated at my ordination service, and was like a father to me in many ways. He taught much about issuing the public appeal, not so much by watching him in the pulpit as by observing his life-style. He never stood on Sunday morning to offer a public appeal without making sure he had offered personal and private appeals during the week. Dr. Swank said, "I can tell you if a man is personally and privately sharing his faith by the passion he displays when he does so publicly on Sunday morning from the pulpit."

Saturday was a workday for Dr. Swank as he would visit in three or four homes to witness for Christ. No wonder he was so effective in his invitations on Sunday. They were the natural overflow of a soul-winner's heart. Many of the men and women who comprised the church leadership he had won to Christ personally in their homes; no wonder the Sagamore Hill church was an evangelistic pacesetter and baptized hundreds of new converts annually for four decades; no wonder either that over one hundred young men sensed God's call to the ministry in that church, and today are preaching the gospel around the world. We were caught up in the passion of a preacher who not only extended the appeal where all could see him but also in the dens and living rooms of the city out of sight to all but his hearers and his Lord.

Ours is life's highest calling. We have the privilege of calling men and women to the Lord Jesus Christ. The pastor not consistently offering the appeal in person will find it awfully difficult to do so publicly in a manner that will produce lasting fruit. It is sheer hypocrisy to offer a public invitation when we seldom or never invite people privately to accept the Lord Jesus. Whether we extend Christ's appeal publicly or privately. . . *make it passionate!*

Chapter 11
Make It Pleasant

If anything ought to be done with a winsome smile and pleasant manner, it is the appeal for people to trust Jesus Christ. We often make the gospel seem offensive because of how we sometimes present it to others. Berating or bullying others into a "decision" does not lead to spiritual success. Neither intimidation nor embarrassment produce lasting commitments. Using undue pressure is not as advantageous as being pleasant in our approach.

The Bible records that the early believers most successful in one-on-one evangelism "enjoyed the favor of all the people" (see Acts 2:47). They were pleasant in their proclamation and winsome in their witness, and many thousands responded to their public and private appeals in the first few months following the birth of the church in Jerusalem.

Too few followers of Christ today are consistently establishing friendships with unsaved people. In our quest to "come out from them and be separate" (2 Cor. 6:17), we have confused insulation from the world with isolation from the world. There is a revealing postscript added at the end of Luke's moving chapter on the nativity.

"And Jesus grew in wisdom and stature, and in favor with God and men" (Luke 2:52). Jesus enjoyed a balanced life. He grew intellectually, physically, spiritually, and *socially*. He grew in "favor with...men." He was gracious and friendly as He approached others.

In fact, he was accused of being "a friend of sinners." Everywhere He went with His appeal He established pleasant relationships, and men and women were caught up in His warm personality. He established relationships at a well one day and in the marketplace the next. He never intimidated nor shamed others into becoming His followers. The church's direst need today is for members to blast outside the four walls of the sanctuary and touch the lives of those in need of Christ, and do it winsomely. Our public appeals on Sunday would assume a new spirit of expectancy if our personal appeals throughout the week were done consistently and pleasantly.

Again I repeat our pattern found in Acts 2:47—that the early believers were "enjoying the favor of all the people." The religious system of the day rejected them. They were a threat to traditional religion which had become stale and institutionalized. The Roman government oppressed them for their refusal to bow before Caesar "as lord." But the people in streets and markets, in towns and villages embraced them. Yes, they enjoyed the "favor" of the people. They were effective in their witness and their worship, and thousands responded to their appeals to accept Christ.

Many Christians have been duped by the erroneous idea that to share Christ with an "outsider" in the marketplace is to invite an unpleasant confrontation. But real Christianity, presented pleasantly and winsomely, is lovely. There is quality about a Spirit-filled, radiant Christian that draws and attracts others and causes them to "[enjoy] favor of all the people." The good news is not as offensive as some of its proponents are! Evangelism in the first-century church was more *caught* than taught, and the same must be true of us if we intend to penetrate the third millennium with the transforming good news of the Lord Jesus Christ.

Not only is it important for us to see we should have favor with the people, but note it is "favor [with] *all* the people" (author's italics). This is what made the appeals of Christ and His first followers so effective. They were not selective in offering the appeal. Remember they were net fishermen and not hook fishermen. Hook fishermen are fishing only for one type of fish. I often put a purple plastic worm on my hook because I am interested only in catching bigmouthed, black bass. I don't want to be bothered with other types of scavenger fish consuming my time. Net fishermen are not selective but catch different kinds of fish.

There is a new idea circulating in church-growth circles that churches should "target" only a certain group of individuals on the socioeconomic scale, most commonly referred to as "baby boomers." While many of these techniques do indeed have much merit and value, when followed to the extreme they can become foreign to the New Testament pattern. The Jerusalem church enjoyed the fellowship of the richest of the rich in Joseph of Arimathea and the poorest of the poor, represented by the widow who gave her all. Since heaven will be like this also, why should we be so prone to compartmentalize here on earth, by race, social standing, or economic status? In order to be God-blessed in our witness we must make our appeals in a cordial manner in order to find "favor [with] all the people." This is good and acceptable in the sight of God, our Savior.

A simple smile has an unbelievably disarming effect. Time and again I have seen a smile become like dynamite to break down a wall of hesitation. I have often seen a smile become a bridge over which our hearers can cross the chasm of unbelief. As you extend the public appeal, step to the side of the pulpit. Don't whip or drive your hearers to the altar. Instead, win them there, lead them there attractively. As you extend the personal appeal in a home, and the time comes to the point of commitment, move to the edge of your seat. With a smile on your face ask the most important question of life: "Would you like to receive the gift of eternal life right now?" More and more people will respond to our public and private appeals when we . . . *make it pleasant!*

Chapter 12
Make It Patient

The public appeal, more commonly referred to as the "invitation," is often the least thought-about and prayed-over part of the entire worship service. For many churches it is a routine portion of the service, a part of long-standing tradition, and extended weekly without any expectancy or enthusiasm on the part of those in the pulpit or in the pew.

It is simply "something we've always done" and is to be "tacked on" at the end of the sermon, usually accompanied by a verse or two of a familiar hymn. This attitude permeating the atmosphere is the very reason it is so often void of visible response. I personally consider the time of appeal the culmination of the worship experience.

Since it presents the perfect opportunity for men and women to act on what they have heard and felt in the service it should be given patiently, allowing the Holy Spirit time to move on the hearts of the hearers, drawing them to Christ. It should be a well-thought-about, planned-for, and prayed-over part of the worship service. Time for the appeal should be allotted and protected so it does not undergo the pressure of time restraints at the end of the service.

Hurried and haphazard appeals seldom result in positive response. The problem arises due to the fact that often
everything in the service has been thought through and
discussed beforehand, *except* the invitation. Those planning the service discuss what hymns would be appropri-
ate, the content of the pastoral prayer, who and what will
comprise the special music, who will give the offertory
prayer, who will make the announcements, what subject
the sermon will address, and even who will pray the
benediction.

Consequently, the appeal is often given no priority and
viewed as a necessary addendum to the sermon. This
attitude carries over from pulpit to pew, and the appeal is
gradually squeezed into a couple of minutes. If the public
appeal is worth doing, it should be done patiently, not
hurriedly.

It is the pastor's responsibility to instill importance and
priority into the public appeal. Those in the pew need to
be taught the necessity of remaining patient, prayerful,
and positive during the appeal. I remember attending a
large church in another state a few years ago. The pastor
preached a masterful message and extended the public
appeal as the scheduled time of the service was nearing
completion. At least two hundred people left through the
back doors as the pastor offered the invitation at the altar.
No wonder there was such little public response. The
distraction of scores of people moving out the back doors
as the pastor called others to the front was overwhelming.

I begin my public appeals with "I am going to ask that
not a single person leave this room unless it is an absolute
emergency. This is God's time of invitation." Quite
frankly, I would much rather people leave in the middle of
my sermon than at the time of the public appeal.

Give the invitation time. Make it a priority. Give it patiently, allowing the Holy Spirit time to do His work of conviction of sin and convincing of Christ's righteousness. Think it through. Plan for it. Pray about it. Make sure you save time for it in the worship service. And above all . . . *make it patient!*

Chapter 13
Make It Public

There is considerable debate today regarding the profitability of the public appeal. While it has been effectively used since the days of the New Testament, some sincerely believe it has no place in corporate worship. Yet, Jesus said, "Whosoever therefore shall confess me before men, him will I confess also before my Father which is in heaven" (Matt. 10:32, KJV). As we study the life of Christ it is noteworthy that Jesus never called anyone to follow Him that He did not do so publicly. There was Nicodemus who came privately to Jesus one night, but when Christ initiated the encounter He always did so publicly. He walked along the shores of Galilee and saw a group of fishermen mending their nets. He looked into the faces of Andrew and Peter, James and John, and said, "Follow me, . . . and I will make you fishers of men" (Matt. 4:19). And they did in front of all their friends and fellow fishermen! They stepped out publicly and followed Jesus.

In Capernaum he encountered Matthew, the tax-collector, sitting at the receipt of customs on a busy workday with several customers and clients around. Jesus spoke those two simple words, "Follow me." And Matthew did in front of all those people who knew him best. When Jesus passed through Jericho it was like a Super Bowl parade. Throngs of people lined the streets for a glimpse of Him. He stopped under a tree, looked up, saw Zacchaeus hiding there watching, and called for him to come down and walk with Him. And Zacchaeus did! In front of everyone. Yes, every time Jesus called men and women to follow Him, He did it publicly. Why? There is an element about our response to a public appeal that helps seal it in our lives. It is simply one of those "tangible intangibles."

No one in church history has been more effective in extending the public appeal than Billy Graham. In its defense he has stated, "Some who are against public evangelistic invitations go to almost any length using the appeal in personal evangelism. If it is right to ask a single sinner to repent and receive the Lord Jesus Christ, why is it not right to ask a whole audience to do the same?" Good question. The public appeal goes hand in hand with the personal appeal. It makes no sense to me to spend thirty minutes explaining the gospel, encouraging others toward it, and exhorting them to receive it as a free gift of God's grace, and then dismissing the crowd without ever giving them an opportunity to do so. If it is right to extend the appeal personally and privately, it is equally correct to offer it publicly.

I attended a graduation exercise recently. Not one of the graduates in cap and gown was embarrassed or ashamed to step out publicly, walk to the front of the auditorium, shake the hand of the principal, and receive their diploma. In fact, many of them were cheered on by their family and friends. Every time I perform a wedding I am reminded of the same principle. The bride and groom walk down the center aisle of the church, unashamedly and unapologetically, to commit their lives to each other openly and publicly. There is a deep sentiment about that public act bringing tremendous joy and encouragement to family and friends, and, at the same time, helping to seal the commitment in the couple's lives. If public appeals are good enough for graduations and weddings, why is that not the case for those making life's greatest commitment to the Lord Jesus Christ? There is a quality about standing publicly for Christ that not only seals the decision in one's own heart but bestows fantastic joy and encouragement on family and friends.

When I extend the invitation I give my hearers an opportunity to do what they love to do—that is, to identify with something. Or, in this case, *Someone!* Have you noticed how many of us like to identify with persons or things? We wear sport shirts with certain little emblems to identify with particular brands; we carry particular automobile insignias on our key chains to identify with a certain make of car. Our belts may have distinctive buckles, and our handbags are often easily identifiable. We wear fraternity pins and school jackets that link us with our alma mater. The public appeal gives people the opportunity to do what they love to do, to identify openly, unashamedly, and publicly with the Lord Jesus Christ.

The public appeal has had a significant place in Christian commitment since the Lord's use of it almost two thousand years ago. We need not excuse it nor apologize for it in our day. In fact, we cannot expect people to stand for Christ outside the four walls of the church in the marketplace, where the world is indifferent and often hostile to the gospel, if they cannot walk down a carpeted aisle of an air-conditioned church around Christians who will rejoice in their decisions for Christ. The public decision helps seal the personal decision which precedes it. Therefore don't be hesitant to . . . *make it public!*

Chapter 14
Make It Premeditated

Some of my readers are engaged in regularly issuing the appeal from the pulpit. I trust most of my readers are seeking to sharpen their skills in presenting the appeal personally or privately. The point I make in this chapter is: the appeal itself should be properly planned for and premeditated. It is not just an afterthought.

Once I have completed my sermon preparation I generally sit back and ask myself a very important question, *So what?* Then I begin to plan and pray about the invitation. I want my appeal to issue from the sermon and be a vital part of it. I seek to somehow, some way melt my message into the truth found in Ephesians 2:8-10 which states, "For it is by grace you have been saved, through faith—and this not from yourselves, it is the gift of God—not by works, so that no one can boast. For we are God's workmanship, created in Christ Jesus to do good works, which God prepared in advance for us to do." As I premeditate on the appeal and plan for it, there are several ideas I want my hearers to understand. First, I want to make it plain about *salvation's outset*. Where does salvation begin? No one can live a Christian life without a clear understanding of its

outset. If we are not right at the beginning we will be
wrong everywhere else. Salvation's outset is in these
words: "For it is by grace you have been saved." Salvation
is not God's response to our good works—it is solely and
entirely of grace, God's unmerited favor. I also want to be
plain about *salvation's outlet* which is found in the next
phrase, "You have been saved, through faith." Faith is the
outlet, the conduit, through which God's grace flows to
man's heart. "Without faith it is impossible to please God"
(Heb. 11:6).

One of the obvious pitfalls to avoid in the public appeal
is the danger that anyone might equate the act of "walking
down an aisle" or "coming to the front" of the stadium
with the miracle of regeneration itself. Thus, we should
not only make plain salvation's outset and outlet, but also
salvation's outcry. It is in these words, "And this not from
yourselves, . . . not by works so that no one can boast."

We are hearing much about America's work ethic today.
Many Japanese are claiming the American worker is lazy
and has no work ethic. There is one place where Ameri-
cans believe strongly in the work ethic, and that is in the
area of eternal salvation! More than ever salvation's outcry
should echo in every appeal to embrace the good news,
"Not from yourselves, . . . not by works!"

As I plan my appeal I also want to be clear regarding
salvation's outlay. Paul continues, reminding us that "it is
the gift of God." Salvation is not a goal to be achieved but
a gift to be received. Failure to grasp this simple truth has
resulted in all sorts of spiritual perversions and given rise
to cults and other false religions. If yours is the sacred task
of issuing the public appeal, make certain the physical act
of responding is differentiated from the reception of the
free gift of God's grace that comes only through faith.

The highest calling and the greatest privilege in life is introducing men and women to the Lord Jesus Christ and extending His appeal to receive the gift of eternal life through faith alone and by His grace. When you plan for this important appeal . . . *make it premeditated!*

Chapter 15
Make It Practical

There is an extremely practical side to extending the invitation. When given properly and prayerfully it is a means to an eternally important end.

My own public appeal is given while my hearers remain seated. At the end of my sermon and without any music I ask them to leave their seats and join me at the front to be included in a prayer. My intention in the public appeal is to build a bridge for those under the Spirit's convicting power to walk across in order to be dealt with on a personal basis.

When the people have responded and are standing at the altar, I voice a prayer and then invite them to follow one of our ministers into our welcome center where we deal with each inquirer on an individual basis and issue a personal appeal. (See Appendix A for a word description of this invitation.) For me the public appeal is a means of achieving the personal appeal. The unsaved are often deeply moved when they see a friend or family member respond to the public appeal. Those who respond seem to serve as escorts and encouragers for others to follow.

I never assume anything at the time of invitation. In our city I speak to several in each service who have never experienced a public invitation to receive Christ as Savior. Consequently, I spell it out in practical terms, telling them exactly what I am asking them to do, for instance, "In a moment I am going to ask you to do something that will take courage. When we bow our hearts in prayer I am going to ask you to stand, leave your seat, and make your way into the aisle. Those next to you will make way for you and will pat you on the back as you go and say, 'God bless you.'

"I am going to ask you to make your way down this aisle and stand with me here at the front. You do not have to worry about what to say. I know why you are coming. And by coming you will be saying, 'I am going to go God's way.' I will meet you here. Many are going to come, and when we all get here I am going to lead in a prayer. After the prayer we want to invite you into the welcome center and give you some Bible study material that will help you. If you come as an inquirer we will lead you to faith in Christ Jesus. Remember, you do not need to worry about what to say. By your coming you will be saying that you are going God's way."

I seek to be as practical as I can at the time of invitation. Put yourself in that man or woman's place in the pew. They have a desire to respond but do not know what to expect. I want them to know exactly what to expect. No surprises! I walk through it with them. They know they are not going to have to say anything to the congregation. They know I am going to lead the prayer, and they will not be embarrassed.

It must be repeated: many public appeals are void of response simply because the hearers are uncertain about what they are being challenged to do. Some preachers come to the end of the sermon and simply say, "Now we're going to stand and sing two verses of hymn number 244. Won't you come?" And the person in the pew is asking himself, *Come where? Come to whom? Come for what reason? Come when?* And he walks out the door without any response to what he has heard and felt in his heart.

A pressing need of our generation is to make Christ's call practical. Jesus talked about the necessity of continually changing wineskins so the wine might be preserved. Old wineskins lost their elasticity and became brittle. When new wine, not fully fermented and still expanding by releasing its gases, was poured into old wineskins, they often burst, and both the wine and skin were lost. However, when new wine was poured into new skins both were preserved.

The wine is the message. It never changes. The wineskins are the methods. They should be constantly changing. For example, we in the church sometimes use a vocabulary that is foreign to those in the marketplace. We try to reach a modern, unchurched world with seventeenth-century English because we are used to it. But the lost person doesn't talk like that. He doesn't ask his secretary, "Wilt thou transcribe this epistle?" No. He says it like the *New International Version,* "Will you take a letter?" Wineskins. If we do not change our clichés the world will never respond.

Watch your words when making the appeal whether publicly or personally. Avoid church clichés. This is why we use the words "welcome center" in describing our "counseling room." It disarms our hearers and conveys a sense of warmth and welcome. It is a bridge instead of a barrier.

As you extend the gospel appeal seek to put yourself in your hearers' shoes. Think like they are thinking. In all our concerns about being passionate and pious, personal, and persuasive . . . *make it practical!*

Chapter 16
Make It Psychological

In this chapter I am not insinuating that we play mind games with our hearers and appeal to them through some sort of mental manipulation. Frankly, we need an outlet, an avenue of response affirming to others our own personal commitment to Jesus Christ. The public appeal provides exactly that. It is psychologically beneficial. There is something about standing on top of the winner's platform at the Olympic Games and hearing your national anthem that helps seal the achievement in the mind forever. And there is something about responding to Christ in public that helps affirm the decision in our lives. Like a public wedding ceremony, a winner's platform, or a graduation exercise, the response to the public appeal can be psychologically therapeutic. By our very makeup and nature we need to make our responses openly and unashamedly.

There is something psychological about making our spiritual decisions open and public. It becomes a mental visual aid that lasts a lifetime. Often those private and personal decisions are soon forgotten, but the response to a public appeal is never forgotten.

I remember well when I was weighing my own personal

call to full-time ministry. It was the summer before my senior year at the university. My lifelong desire was to attend law school and spend my life arguing cases before judge and jury in the courtroom. That particular summer, as I began to sense that God had other plans for me, I began to vacillate from day to day about what I should do. I came to the place where I knew I could find no joy in anything but vocational ministry and was fairly confident it was God's will for my life. Yet, I still wavered back and forth from day to day. Only when I made public my calling was my mind made up once and for all—and I never again looked back. Although that was over twenty years ago I still, in my mind's eye, can see myself in a white turtleneck sweater and gray slacks standing in front of my home church making my decision public. Psychologically, making my call public helped seal it forever in my heart and mind.

Public appeals are also psychologically stimulating and challenging to those who observe them. I often acknowledge men and women in our church who lead others to Christ and come with them to the front in the moment of public appeal. It causes many others to think, *If Bill or Tom or Mary or Kathy can bring someone to Jesus then I can, too.* When children respond to the appeal, I often remind my hearers that Jesus explained if any of us were to follow after Him we have to come like little children in simple childlike faith.

Psychologists in our city and on our staff are quick to point out the positive benefits of the public appeal. Impulses we have to follow Christ will diminish unless they are acted upon soon. The public appeal gives us an opportunity, in the words of the ancient proverb, "to strike while the iron is hot." It is my personal observation that men and women are less apt to respond the second or third time around. In fact, Paul in the Ephesian letter states that the heart becomes harder and more calloused until we reach a point when, although God still calls, we can no longer hear, due to the hardening of hearts resulting from repeatedly neglecting Christ's appeal. There is a psychological urgency about the appeal that calls on us to respond. Carpe diem—"seize the day!"

This principle holds true in the parlor as well as in the public arena. As you share the good news of eternal life it is vital to give people the opportunity of letting others know of and share in their newfound joy. So when you extend the appeal publicly or privately, . . . *make it psychological!*

Chapter 17
Make It Prayerful

Perhaps the most discussed entree on the menu of Christian growth and outreach is prayer. Yet, many times it is also the least ordered. Prayer is the battlefield of the Christian life, especially when we are "drawing the net" and inviting men and women to embrace the Lord Jesus as their personal Savior. It is difficult to win the war if we have no idea where the battle is being fought. Of all the other subjects addressed in this volume, none is of greater importance than the need of a prayer-saturated appeal.

In order to pray effectively for the lost, it is imperative for us to grasp a basic scriptural understanding of why an individual is without Christ in the first place. Behind the simple fact that the lost person has not received the gospel is the reality that he is not only bound but also blinded by "the god of this world," Satan. He is bound by the devil. In the words of the apostle Paul, we should pray that lost men and women might "come to their senses and escape from the trap of the devil, who has taken them captive to do his will" (2 Tim. 2:26). As we pray for others in times of appeal we should be aware that in this battle lost men and women are bound and blinded by him as well.

Paul also says, "And even if our gospel is veiled, it is veiled to those who are perishing. The god of this age has blinded the minds of unbelievers, so that they cannot see the light of the gospel of the glory of Christ, who is the image of God" (2 Cor. 4:3-4). Thus, two things need to happen before a person can be saved. The binding and the blinding must be broken. This occurs in intercession. Remember, "The weapons we fight with are not the weapons of the world. On the contrary, they have divine power to demolish strongholds. We demolish arguments and every pretension that set themselves up against the knowledge of God, and we take captive every thought to make it obedient to Christ" (10:4-5).

Thus we have the power in prayer to move into the spiritual realm and knock down the stronghold in which the devil has a lost person bound and blinded. Consequently our aim in prayer at the time of appeal should not be in the direction of the particular individual for whom we are concerned but at the devil himself! This is what our Lord did in Caesarea Philippi. After Jesus instructed the disciples about His ensuing death, Peter, with good intentions, sought to divert Him from the cross. Jesus said, "Get thee behind me, Satan" (Matt. 16:22, KJV). He was not addressing himself to Peter. He realized there was a power behind Peter motivating him to say what he had said, and Jesus dealt directly with the devil.

Paul followed Christ's example when, upon being tormented by a fortune teller, "he turned around and [spoke] to the spirit" (Acts 16:18). Prayer is the true battlefield in "the valley of decision" when people are weighing in the balance of eternity their ultimate destiny. Our job as intercessors, when the appeal is being extended, is to "demolish strongholds," the binding and the blinding which keep men and women from a saving knowledge of Christ for "no one can enter a strong man's house and carry off his possessions unless he first ties up the strong man" (Mark 3:27).

Every service as I extend the invitation hundreds of intercessors are praying and "demolishing strongholds" at the same time. If we could only realize what is going on in the unseen world around us! Think about it the next time you are in a corporate worship experience and a public appeal is extended. If only you had a television monitor that could pick up color pictures traveling through the room in the unseen realm, or you had a radio on which you could hear all sorts of sound and music circling all around you in the unseen realm. There is also in this unseen, spiritual realm a gigantic battle being waged for the souls of men and women who sit among you.

This is why prayer must be a priority when drawing the net. As I verbally extend the public appeal I have taught my people to pray for and demolish three primary strongholds. There is the stronghold of *pride*. Pride keeps more people from responding to Jesus Christ than anything else. Pride, the *big I*, the perpendicular pronoun. Those in this stronghold are more concerned about what others think than what God thinks. In times of public appeals there is also the stronghold of *presumption*. Some do not respond to the appeal because they are presuming upon some "decision" made years ago but which resulted in no transformation of life. Many people enter a Christless eternity because they "presume" upon a false decision.

The other major stronghold I have taught my people to demolish in prayer is *procrastination*. Some do not respond to Christ's appeal because they think there will be adequate time in the future, so they postpone the call. They put it off. When this stronghold is demolished it helps others realize that not to decide is to decide! Through the years it has thrilled me to see over one hundred people every month responding to our public appeals, primarily because of an army of prayer warriors who pray for the demolition of strongholds in every service.

Prayer must be our priority in public and private appeals. In our evangelism training ministry we go out to share Christ in groups of three. We pray before we leave; we pray in the car as we go; and we pray on the porch as we await the answer to the doorbell. Once inside, as the trainer is sharing and extending the personal appeal, the other two team members are in constant prayer demolishing strongholds.

Our church is involved in the Watchman Prayer Ministry and every hour around the clock, every day of the week, every week of the year, four people are making intercession and continually praying for the tearing down of strongholds in our city. Every Saturday morning scores of our people meet in our worship center, kneel, and pray at each of the almost 4,000 seats for the individual who will sit there the following morning. Can you imagine the encouragement that is to me personally when I address the crowds on Sunday, knowing that everyone has been prayed for and strongholds are being flattened?

Our people have also been taught to pick out an individual in the congregation at the beginning of worship and pray for them during the entire service. Every week our people experience the joy of answered prayer as persons whom they have never met respond to the appeal. I seek to do this myself. Perhaps during the song service I will pick out a man I have never seen and pray for him throughout the service and into my message. Yes, prayer is the battlefield, and it is impossible to win a war if we are unaware of where the battle is being fought.

Of all the techniques that could be addressed, and of all the tried and proven principles of refining the public or personal appeal, there is nothing more needed than to bathe the appeal in intercessory prayer. Whether it is yours to extend the appeal publicly or personally, above all, . . . *make it prayerful!*

Chapter 18
Make It Perpetual

One subtle danger of the public appeal is that some people may think it is the best, and perhaps only, forum in which people may decide for Jesus Christ. Fifty years ago in the rural areas of our land, most every church had a "protracted" two-week revival in July or August each year. It was *the* time to "get saved."

If certain individuals went through the "protracted meeting" without responding and being converted, the people would comment to one another, "Let's pray and maybe next August he'll (she'll) be saved!" Many churches even today make a tremendous mistake in thinking the invitation ends when we leave the church building.

The appeal to follow Christ should be *perpetual*. It should permeate the environment of the entire church and all its ministries. In fact, no organization in the church has a right to exist unless its underlying goals and motives are to lead people to a saving knowledge of the Lord Jesus Christ. More than all else we must permeate our churches with a fresh, new commitment to the old and grand commandment to make disciples of everyone everywhere.

Many people in church mission organizations drive past

over a hundred mission opportunities to attend their church and then talk about how concerned they are for those in Africa or Third-World countries. This is a sad commentary on missions in the New Testament sense. We cannot play leap frog with the Great Commission.

It begins in our own "Jerusalem." The concept of casting and "drawing the net" should permeate everything we do as a church. We have almost one hundred ongoing ministries in our fellowship in Fort Lauderdale, and each presents people with the opportunity to receive Christ as their personal Savior. We minister to hundreds of cancer patients through our cancer support ministry with the underlying motive to present a personal appeal to receive the Lord. Our literacy ministry is training scores of people to read. It is marvelous to see a new world open up to so many. But our primary purpose is to make a personal appeal to receive the Lord. We have scores of ministries, but we have only one purpose, and that is to fulfill the Great Commission by making, marking, and maturing followers of the Lord Jesus Christ.

The appeal to follow Christ is not merely what the preacher does once or twice a week from the pulpit. It is something that should permeate our church ministries and the life-style of our members. Quite frankly, many of those who walk forward in our church have already responded to a personal appeal from one of our members who "draws the net" as a way of life in the marketplace day by day.

In our church this appeal to others saturates all we do. Our committees make all of our church's decisions on the basis of those who are "not here yet." We encourage our people to build relationships with lost people. Jesus did. They called Him a "friend of sinners." I wonder if the

leadership of many modern churches has ever been accused of such. Wherever our Lord went He made personal
appeals to those in need, whether they were at a well or in
a marketplace. I continue to impress on our people the
importance of making our decisions and planning our
programs for those who are "not here yet." Many churches
make their decisions on the basis of those already there or,
worse yet, who have been there for forty years. We will
never impact our world with the gospel with public appeals. A spirit of evangelism, and personal and private
appeals, must permeate our churches and fellowships as a
life-style.

As we approach and enter this third millennium, there
are open doors of opportunity all around us. Let's make
our decisions and exist for those not in the family as yet,
and as we make the appeal publicly or privately, let's . . .
make it perpetual!

Chapter 19
Make It Pertinent

The appeal should flow from the body of the gospel presentation and relate to the content of the message. Many of those extending the appeal have difficulty making a smooth transition into the invitation to receive Christ.

Sudden and abrupt transitions from the presentation to the appeal distract the hearer and divert the flow of the speaker. When presenting the message of salvation to others in a personal, one-on-one fashion, I have found transitional questions to be disarming and extremely helpful in maintaining the flow of the conversation. When the presentation is concluded it is helpful to ask a qualifying question such as one suggested by D. James Kennedy of Coral Gables Presbyterian Church and founder of Evangelism Explosion: "Does this make sense to you?" On receiving an answer in the affirmative, the transition has been made, and the more pertinent question for commitment can then be asked, "Would you like to receive the free gift of eternal life?"

In our pulpit appeals the invitation should always issue from the thesis of the sermon. My own preaching style is expository, verse-by-verse exposition through books of the Bible. Consequently, I seldom preach what one might refer to as a "hard-core, fire-and-brimstone" evangelistic sermon. But I always make a strong evangelistic appeal which I seek to make pertinent to the message and issue straight from it.

For example, I recently preached through Paul's letter to Philemon. In a particular message I was dealing with the subject of interpersonal relationships in the home, the office, and in the social arena. When it came time for the appeal I made my transition from information to invitation by saying, "There are only three relationships in life. There is an *upward* expression. That is a relationship with God. This is what makes us different from animals. We have the capacity to connect with God Himself through Jesus Christ. Second, there is the *inward* expression. We have a relationship with ourselves which involves self-worth, self-respect, and self-love.

"Finally, there is an *outward* expression. We have a relationship with others, whether in the home, at school, in the office, or wherever we interact with other people. The truth is, we will never be properly related to others until we are properly related to ourselves. If we have no real self-love or self-respect we project that into destructive relationships with others. Jesus was on target when He said we should 'love our neighbor as we love ourself.'

"But we must go a step further to find the ultimate truth: we will never be properly related to ourselves unless we are properly related to God by receiving the free gift of eternal life made possible for us through His Son. Only then can we realize how indescribably valuable we are to God and really begin to feel good about ourselves.

"So, the only way to have positive, profitable interpersonal relationships with others is to have self-worth and self-respect. The only way true self-worth is acquired is in knowing God through the Lord Jesus Christ."

Although the body of this particular message was not evangelistic in nature the transition to the evangelistic appeal was made so it issued out of the sermon and was pertinent to it.

No matter the subject of the sermon, it can be applied evangelistically. Take, for example, a message on world peace. Jesus has called us to be "peacemakers," not just peace lovers. That is—we are to be promoters of unity. The transition to the evangelistic appeal might be made like this, "We will never have peace on a global level until we have peace on a continental level; we will never have peace on a continental level until we have peace on a national level; we will never have peace on a national level until we have peace on a state level; we will never have peace on a state level until we have peace on a county level. We will never have peace on a county level until we have peace on a city level; we will never have peace on a city level until we have peace on a neighborhood level; we will never have peace on a neighborhood level until we have peace on our street—we will never have peace on our street until we have peace on our block; we will never have peace on our block until we have peace in our home; we will never have peace in our home until there is peace in our hearts. And there will never be peace in our hearts until we have made peace with God through our Lord Jesus Christ!"

Now the stage is set for the evangelistic appeal—pertinent to the sermon and issuing from it.

It matters not what we preach. We can always find a way to make a smooth transition and direct our hearers to the cross. Once I delivered a message on the subject of friendship, what it means to be a true friend. I found my transition to the appeal in a poem written by an unknown author that follows:

> My friend I stand in judgment now
> And feel that you're to blame somehow.
> On earth I walked with you by day,
> And never did you point the way.
>
> You knew the Lord in truth and glory;
> But never did you tell the story.
> My knowledge then was very dim,
> You could have led me on to Him.
>
> Though we lived together here on earth,
> You never mentioned a second birth.
> And now I stand this day condemned
> Because you failed to mention Him.
>
> You taught me many things, that's true.
> I called you "friend" and trusted you.
> But now I learn that it's too late.
> You could have kept me from this fate.
>
> We walked by day and talked by night;
> And yet, you showed me not the light.
> You let me live and love and die;
> But knew I'd never live on high.
>
> Yes, I called you "friend" in life
> And trusted you through joy and strife,
> And yet, on coming to this dreadful end
> No longer can I call you . . . FRIEND!

In an interesting, but nonconfrontational, way, I had made my transition from the body of my sermon on friendship to the launching pad of the evangelistic appeal. Transitions are of vital importance in keeping the attention and interest of our hearers.

Whether you are privileged to offer Christ's appeal publicly from the pulpit or personally with a friend, make sure it issues out of the thesis of the presentation and . . . *make it pertinent!*

Chapter 20
Make It Plenary

While the personal, private appeal has the profession of faith as its singular focus, the public appeal is more all-encompassing and plenary in nature. In the corporate worship setting there are many and varied needs to which we should appeal.

As I view my own congregation and seek to fill their needs week by week, I am aware there are many of my hearers who are there out of inquiry or curiosity and have yet to embrace the gospel. There are also those who have accepted Christ during the week as our people extended the personal appeal to them. They now need to make their decisions public. There are others with a need to move their church membership and become a part of our "team."

Still others do not know what they need to do or how to respond. All they know is that life has lost its purpose and direction. The something they think they need is really Someone! We cannot entertain false assumptions that our hearers understand what we are encouraging them to do. This is not the case. We must spell it out and be plenary in our approach. It takes me about five or six minutes to do this at the beginning of my own public appeals, but I leave no doubt in the hearers' minds about what I am asking them to do and how I am asking them to respond.

For example, there are those who need to accept the free gift of eternal life. I generally appeal to them in the following manner: "I know there are many of you here who have never trusted in Jesus Christ alone for your salvation. If you were to die today you do not know where you would spend eternity. In just a moment I am going to ask you to leave your seat and come and stand with me here at the front. By your coming you will be saying, 'I want to know Jesus Christ.' Many are going to come and when we get here I am going to lead in a prayer. If you are coming as an inquirer we want to sit down with you and lead you to faith in Jesus Christ." Those who need to be converted now know what they can do about it and what to expect when they respond.

Others in my congregation have already invited Christ to be their personal Savior, but they need to make a public pledge of their life to Him for reasons discussed in previous chapters.

I generally appeal to this group in the following manner: "There are others of you who have already opened your heart to Christ, perhaps this week, last week, last month, or whenever, who now need to make a public pledge. I am going to ask you to join the others who are coming and by your coming you will be saying, 'I am going to go God's way by openly, unashamedly, and publicly identifying with Him.' Jesus said if we would confess Him before men He would, in turn, confess us before the Father in heaven. There is something about a public decision that will help solidify it in your life. When Christ called people to follow Him He always did so publicly. It is the right thing to do."

Still others in the congregation are uncertain of their own salvation and need assurance. To these I might add the following: "Many of you are honest enough to say, 'I really am unsure about whether I am a Christian.' God doesn't want you to wonder and worry from one day to the next whether you are saved or lost. In fact, He says the Bible was written that you may 'know that you have eternal life.' "He says the experience of salvation is like going from death into life or darkness into light. How can you go from a dark room into a light room and not know it? How can you pass from death into life and not know it? God has not made it hard to be saved. In fact, He says that if any of us will come to Him we must come in simple, childlike faith, trusting in Him alone for salvation.

"If you are uncertain you can settle it today. I am going to ask you to join the others who are coming in just a moment. By your coming you will be saying, 'I'm not sure I have received eternal life, but I want to be, and I want to settle it, once and for all, this morning right now.' I will look for you to be first, and I'll meet you here at the front. We have some material to give you that will help you, and we want to sit down with you and lead you to the assurance of your salvation." Those of my hearers who have been wrestling with a lack of assurance now know they are not alone, and they no longer have to be afraid to admit it and to seek guidance.

There are yet others in my congregation who are church members and followers of the Lord Jesus Christ but who are no longer active in their previous church fellowships. Perhaps they have moved to our area or are attending from other churches for whatever reason. They have a need to unite with our fellowship. To these I publicly appeal in the following manner: "Many of you are Christians but are no longer active in a local church. This is where you are now eating your spiritual food, and it is now time for you to come out of the shadows and put on the uniform of church membership. You have thought about it, planned on it, prayed about it, and the only thing left is to *just do it*. I am going to ask you to join the others who are going to come in just a moment. By your coming you will be saying, 'I am going to put my life in this church and serve God in it and through it.' Be the first, and by your coming you will be an escort for the many who need to know the Lord Jesus." We are ministering in a day when people are not "joiners," as in the past. So, in our plenary appeals we must encourage this group to lead the way.

When the public appeal is given it needs to be plenary. Many are lamenting the fact that more young people are not surrendering to God's call to the ministry, and yet there are thousands of churches where the appeal to ministry has not been heard from the pulpit in years! Our congregation currently has thirty adults serving Christ on foreign mission fields and dozens of others who have gone out from us in church-related ministries. We believe in challenging our people from the pulpit and "calling out the called" through the public appeal.

If it is your privilege to offer the public appeal, be certain you are plain, that you spell it out, and that you . . . *make it plenary!*

Chapter 21
Make It Perceptive

Drawing the net demands a special sensitivity to the Holy Spirit. Those of us who issue the invitation must be perceptive to the Spirit. There are times in our corporate worship when I sense a special moving of the Lord on His people, and I offer the appeal at that time.

For example, it has happened on occasion that I have done so early in the service before the message was even preached. Once during a solo before the sermon it was as though God Himself walked into the room. Most everyone seemed to recognize it. The man singing continued with deep emotion as tears of gratitude rushed down his cheeks.

A holy hush descended upon the congregation. It was not time for the sermon but the moment to acknowledge God's presence and give opportunity for a response. In capsule form I shared the good news and extended the public appeal. Many responded, all "before the message." There have been other occasions in our worship service when men and women, under the convicting power of God, have left their seats in the very middle of the sermon and found their way to the altar. On more than one of these occurrences, I have stopped the message, offered an appeal, and then continued with the sermon. The simple point I am making is that we do not always have to give the appeal like we have always done before. Be sensitive. Be perceptive to the leading of the Holy Spirit, whether you are in the pulpit, on a plane, or in the parlor.

There are many new, innovative ways to offer Christ's appeal in the worship setting. Don't be predictable—be perceptive. In Fort Lauderdale we extend the appeal in various ways at different times. When we give the invitation on Sunday mornings at the conclusion of one of our grand celebration worship experiences, we do so without any singing. The people remain seated throughout the appeal. (If someone is positioned in the middle of an aisle and feels a need to respond it becomes a mental barrier when everyone is standing, singing a hymn. In order for him to move into the aisle to come forward, everyone in the pew has to step out to let him pass. In his own mind he sees this as an inconvenience to people he does not even know. Thus, he often postpones the prompting of his heart. On the other hand, if those next to him are seated and in a spirit of prayer, it is much easier for him to slip past them into the aisle and to the altar.) As I extend the Sunday morning public appeal (see Appendix A for detailed invitation), I ask the people to stand, make their way into the aisle, and join me at the front while the entire congregation bows in prayer.

It never ceases to amaze me how, in the quietness of the moment, people begin to respond from all over the building. Once we are gathered at the front I lead in a word of prayer and invite those who have responded into our "welcome center," a room near the auditorium designed with a reception area and several adjacent small rooms where a trained counselor deals individually with each respondee. Those joining our church from other congregations are asked to share with the counselor their personal salvation testimony. We feel it is imperative and important to do our best in assuring a regenerate church membership.

In our "Saturday Night Live" worship experience, designed to attract those who have been out of church for years, we extend the appeal in a totally different manner. At the end of my sermon when I am seeking to "tie a bow" onto the conclusion of the message, I call the congregation's attention to a particular green card in the pew rack at each seat. The card is entitled "I Am Interested in Knowing More About Spiritual Things." It has a place for one's name and address, a place to "check" that they would like to know more about spiritual things, and some brief instructions regarding an invitation to meet us in the welcome center for a reception immediately following the service.

I challenge them to take the card and meet me and others in a designated place upon the conclusion of the service. This is an adaptation of what the evangelist of the past, Charles Finney, used to call the "anteroom." We have found this to be an effective tool for more contemporary worship.

Our midweek worship service presents a different approach and appeal. We conclude our service on Wednesday evenings with a call for prayer for the sick. We invite those who request prayer for themselves personally to come and kneel at our prayer altars where our elders pray for one another. The emphasis is for those who not only need God's touch physically but also may be sick in the soulish realm of emotions (brokenhearted, depressed, and the like), and also those who may request prayer for their spiritual needs.

Since we are made up of spirit, soul, and body we seek to be holistic in our prayer approach. Once these have gathered and are being prayed for, I then say to the rest of the congregation, "I know many of you know someone who needs prayer at this altar, but they are not here requesting it. Perhaps they cannot be. Maybe they are sick physically and in the hospital. In a moment you will want to come and kneel in their place, as it were, and be an intercessor for them. Perhaps you know someone sick in soul, brokenhearted, depressed, or just emotionally strung out, and they are not here requesting prayer for themselves. In just a moment you will want to come and kneel in their place and intercede in their behalf.

"Or perhaps you know someone who is sick spiritually or spiritually dead without Christ. They are not here tonight calling on the Lord to save them, but in a moment you will want to come and kneel in their place and become an intercessor for them." We then sing a brief chorus while these people move to the altar. Now we have a large group of people on their knees in prayer.

After I lead in prayer I say, "Now before we return to our seats I know there are many of you who would say, 'I am not sure I have eternal life, but I'd like to, and I'd like to settle it tonight.' While we continue in a spirit of prayer if that is your case, would you just lift your hand quickly and put it down?" The inquirer has now admitted his need, and I then make a smooth transition into inviting him or her to move immediately to the welcome center where we can deal on a personal basis with the need of their heart.

Everytime our church meets we give people an opportunity to respond to the call of Christ, though we do it in many different ways and seek to keep from becoming routine and predictable. Our church is located downtown, in the heart of our city, and we have a large business persons' Bible study luncheon each Tuesday. At each table there are cards to register everyone in attendance. On each card is a small box in the lower right corner. At the end of my message I close in prayer and give my hearers the opportunity to open their lives to Christ in the privacy of their own prayer.

At the conclusion, I ask those who have prayed to receive Christ simply to make a mark in the little box on their registration card. I assure them that no one will contact them in any way unless they request it. I do tell them that I will collect the cards and send them a personal, private letter the next day with some Bible study materials and instructions on how to follow through on their decision for Christ. This approach has been most successful in our fellowship with the business and professional community.

This chapter could continue indefinitely with different methods of offering the appeal. My point is simply that we need to be perceptive to our crowds and the Holy Spirit. In short, don't be continually repetitive and predictable in your approach. We don't always have to sing four verses of "Just as I Am" and pressure people through all sorts of manipulation into a response. Our regulars will be prone to lose their sense of expectancy if we fall into a routine that never changes. Newcomers will wonder what they should do. Many of us assume the ones who really need to respond understand our invitation system, and we end up merely talking back and forth to ourselves each Sunday with little visible response.

Be flexible. Be perceptive. It may surprise some of us

that many of the great soul-winning churches in past generations, as well as our own, never have extended public appeals. Charles Haddon Spurgeon of London's Metropolitan Tabernacle didn't. One of the tremendous soul-winning churches in America is the Coral Ridge Presbyterian Church here in Fort Lauderdale, and my good friend and fellow pastor, D. James (Jim) Kennedy, doesn't extend the public appeal like I do. Bill Hybels, pastor of the largest and fastest-growing church in the Western world, Willow Creek Church in the Chicago area, does not extend a public appeal. However, the evangelistic and growing churches in Southern Baptist fellowships make effective use of the public appeal. The point is, we do not all have to do it the same way.

I personally believe there is considerable merit in the invitation system as we know it, but more and more I am realizing there are different and innovative ways to approach and extend it. Whether it is your privilege to offer the appeal to others publicly or privately... *make it perceptive!*

Chapter 22
Make It Presumptive

In challenging each other to make the invitation presumptive, we mean that it should be logical, it should make sense. Webster defines the word as the "ground lending probability to belief."

In short, don't try to be someone you are not when you issue the appeal. Be yourself. This volume offers many suggestions and variations in how we may extend Christ's appeal to others in private and public settings, but when all is said and done, and you come to the bottom line, be yourself. Be as wise as young David who knew he could not confront the giant in Saul's armor. It just didn't fit. Use your own "weapons" as you extend the appeal, and if something you read or hear doesn't "fit" don't "wear" it.

Wherever God has placed us to advance His kingdom we should identify with the interests of the people. My first pastorate was in Hobart, Oklahoma, a wheat-farming community in Southwestern Oklahoma. During my tenure there a young man was called to pastor one of the smaller churches in a rural area. He became notorious for using detailed sermonic illustrations of such things as nuclear fission, genetic engineering, and a host of other subjects about which those good and godly farmers didn't have a clue. Nor did the young pastor, I might add! The privilege of extending Christ's appeal in His behalf calls for credibility and common sense. Be natural. Talk the language of your people. Meet them at the point of their own interest, and it will go far in building the bridge to a winsome witness.

Jesus always appealed to an individual at the point of his or her particular interest. To the butcher He became the "Lamb of God." To the baker He was the "Bread of life." To the candlestick maker He was the "Light of the world." He appealed to the three wise men at the point of their interest. They were astronomers and interested in the study of the stars. What did He do? He caught them with a star that led them to Bethlehem.

Most of the disciples were engaged in the fishing business around the Sea of Galilee. The Lord made His public appeal to them at the point of their interest. He said, "Follow me and I will make you fishers of men" (Matt. 4:19). Later, in Samaria at Jacob's Well, He met a woman who had ventured out in the heat because her present interest was in the water business. He made His personal appeal by speaking to her at the point of her particular need and interest. He spoke of "living water" (John 4:10). Wherever our Lord went He never tried to become someone or something He was not and always made His appeal to others according to their particular interests.

Make it natural. Be yourself. Sense the needs of others. You are on special assignment from God, and somewhere there is someone to reach for Christ that no one can reach quite like you can. It doesn't matter whether you pastor the county-seat church, in the suburbs, in the country, full time or bivocational, or whether you serve Christ in a lay capacity. Whoever you may be or whatever you may do, be yourself, and God will make you what He wants you to be. In short, as you extend the appeal be logical and . . . *make it presumptive!*

Chapter 23
Make It Punctual

While many effective pastor-evangelists and lay evangelists of the past have been strong proponents of the long, extended, and protracted invitation, I personally am not of their persuasion. I believe that once the message of redemption has been adequately and persuasively presented the appeal which follows should be punctual.

I have read and heard of those who have sung nine or ten stanzas of an invitation hymn, even though there is no public response. A study of the churches in our day who are winning the greatest numbers to Christ seldom extend long invitations. There is a signal difference in today's evangelistic churches and those of the preceding generation.

In the past, church members would visit people on church invitation nights and encourage them to "come hear our preacher." And they would. The preacher would preach an evangelistic message, extend a long, protracted appeal, and those who would baptize 300 converts a year would lead the churches in our own denomination. Today dozens of our churches exceed these figures. What's the difference? We have discovered something. Today we train our lay people in such programs as Evangelism Explosion or Continued Witness Training, and they reach out to others not by saying, "Come hear my preacher," but they share the good news of Christ and offer a personal appeal to trust Christ on the spot. These witnesses often sit in church the next Sunday with those whom they have personally won to Christ, and when the public appeal is extended they readily respond by making a public pledge.

Not a Sunday goes by in my own public appeals that our men and women are not walking side by side at the time of invitation with those they have personally led to Christ. I venture to say that 90 percent of the adults who make public professions of faith in our worship service do so because one of our members has personally led them to faith in Christ. I could preach Sunday on the fact that there is life on Mars and still see public professions because people have already been won and made ready through a personal appeal. Consequently, I seek to make the public appeal punctual and to the point.

It is important in the appeal to come to the point (See appendix A.) Stay on track! Some make the mistake of coming to the very moment of "drawing the net," and then they take off down some side street on a tangent. We often lose our hearers at this point. It can happen in a time of personal appeal when a question from out of nowhere causes us to "chase a rabbit." Effective and lasting appeals are most generally punctual and to the point. This should not be confused with becoming robotic and mechanical in our appeals. Again, we are talking about being sensitive to the Holy Spirit and, at the same time, sensitive to the responses of our hearers. When God is at work and there is the obvious moving of the Spirit in our midst, the appeal should be extended, keeping in tune with His leading.

When we extend to others Christ's invitation to salvation we should keep it to the point and . . . *make it punctual!*

Chapter 24
Make It Proficient

In the Kingdom's business we should show excellence in all we do. Quality should be the name of the game, especially in our most important task of advancing the Kingdom of God in the place where we live.

Those called to extend the evangelistic appeal should be continually striving to make it better and sharpen their skills. In the economy of God, good is the enemy of the best. Often every aspect in the worship service is given a quality-control check—except the public appeal. In many minds it is simply a given fixture relegated to its place at the end of the sermon as a sort of "sacred cow," yet never given creative thought or attention.

We make certain the music is of a quality nature, the sermon is fine-tuned, and the entire service flows from the "call to worship" to the benediction. But seldom do many of us put quality control into the time of public appeal.

Look at the world around us. Major corporations spend an incredible amount of quality time and training teaching their sales forces how to close a deal. A recent best-selling book was entitled *The Art of Closing the Deal*. All the time spent on information and presentation can never suffice for quality in the time of commitment. Salespersons of all kinds and types are well trained in the art of drawing the net in their respective professions. Yet this very element is often overlooked in the training of those preparing for the ministry. It is inconceivable, yet a reality, that one can graduate from certain seminaries across our country without having been required to take a single course in personal evangelism, much less be trained in the art of "drawing the net."

Whether it is your joy to offer the appeal publicly or personally, study it, refine it, stay on the cutting edge and . . . *make it proficient!*

Chapter 25
Make It Provocative

Nothing we do should be more alluring, more captivating, more inviting, or more provocative than the appeal to others to become followers of the Lord Jesus Christ. There are many ways in which we can break out of the mold, and cause our personal, as well as public, appeals to capture the attention of our hearers. We want to arouse their curiosity and whet their appetite to want to know more and to act on what they are hearing.

As we study the life of our Lord and how He appealed to others, we find that Jesus had an uncanny ability not only to analyze people's concern but to arouse their curiosity. Consider, for example, His encounter with the woman at the well (John 4). By the simple act of talking with her He demolished social, religious, racial, and political barriers which existed in first-century Middle-eastern culture. He aroused her curiosity by speaking to her about "living water" and caused her to ask a question, "Sir. . . . Where can you get this living water?" (vv. 10-11) His provocative approach caused her to ask Him a question, and that is vitally important as we make a personal appeal.

When the inquirer takes the initiative to ask a question

much of the pressure seems to go out of the encounter. I have seen this happen many times in my own personal experience. I have been privileged to share Christ with many people on airplanes. However, I have found I am at a distinct disadvantage as soon as my newfound friend asks my profession, which often comes early on. So, instead of letting my seat-mate know up front I am a minister, I seek to arouse his curiosity to the extent he will ask me a question.

It often happens this way. I am seated on a plane, and someone takes the seat next to me. We exchange smiles, pleasantries, and names. And then invariably it happens. He asks, "What do you do for a living?" And I reply, "I am in the business of telling men and women how to make life's most important discovery!" Then I begin to ignore him and continue reading my book or magazine. It hasn't failed yet. In the course of the flight, usually when the meal is served, he will ask, "All right, what is it?"

I reply, "What is what?"

And, with a smile he asks, "What is life's greatest discovery?"

"I'm glad you asked, and I'll be glad to tell you."

I have aroused his curiosity. He has taken the initiative to ask a question. All the pressure is gone as I begin to share the plan of salvation with him and make a personal appeal for him to put his faith and trust in Jesus Christ in order to make what is, indeed, life's greatest discovery.

We cannot create a spiritual interest in a person. Only the Holy Spirit can do that, for no one has ever truly come to Jesus Christ who was not first drawn by the Father (see John 6:44). But we can be His instruments to arouse curiosity and share Jesus Christ in the power of the Holy Spirit while leaving the results to God. It is important for us to remember that when God is working He is working on both ends of the spectrum. If he leads a Philip to the Gaza desert He will have an Ethiopian there ready to hear and receive the good news. If he leads a Peter to Caesarea he will have a Cornelius there ready to hear and receive the good news. If he leads our Lord to go out of His way and through Samaria to a well, He will have a woman there ready to hear and receive the good news. And if he leads you and me to some particular place at some particular time it will be because He desires us to be His hand extended in passing the cup of living water. We cannot create spiritual interest in another person, but we can be His instrument to arouse curiosity and open the door for the gospel presentation.

Since it is my particular calling to offer the public appeal with regularity, I seek to arouse the curiosity of the congregation at different times during the course of the worship service, as I pray toward and plan for the time of invitation. Early in the service, when we welcome our guests, I may say something to the effect, "Some of you have come here unaware that this will be the most important hour of your life, for this morning you are going to make life's most important discovery and leave here in a few minutes with a brand-new life and a new beginning!"

I have aroused their curiosity and given them something to think about as they hear the music and listen to the message. Then I tie the statement back in at the time of the public appeal. The same but varied approach can be made in the personal appeal as illustrated earlier in this chapter. After the gospel presentation, and just before I ask for commitment in the personal appeal, I have found benefit in qualifying the presentation by asking, "Does this make sense to you?" This gives my hearer the oppor-

tunity to affirm the truth and logic of the gospel and paves
the way for the commitment question. "Would you like to
receive the free gift of eternal life right now?"

Upon an affirmative answer I am then privileged to lead
my friend in a prayer of salvation. (See appendix B.)

I am convinced more people would be responsive to the
gospel if more of us would make the appeal in an alluring
and inviting manner. As you extend Christ's appeal personally on a plane or publicly from a pulpit...*make it
provocative!*

Chapter 26
Make It Pervasive

The public appeal has been a regular fixture in many evangelical churches for so long it can become compartmentalized and roboticly administered at a set time following the sermon and preceding the benediction—and, unfortunately, with little expectancy and anticipation. The public appeal must become more of an attitude than a mere activity in worship. It should permeate the entire worship experience from beginning to end. I personally begin the attitude of the appeal before the service begins, continue it throughout the service, extend it after the message, and eventually dismiss the people with it on their minds. The public appeal should be pervasive.

I actually begin the public appeal thirty minutes before each service. I spend this valuable preservice time walking up and down the aisles of the auditorium, greeting the very people to whom I will make the appeal later in the service. This is a splendid opportunity to speak to scores of people, shake their hands, and touch their lives. Every week someone will motion for me to come by their pew and will introduce me to a friend they have led to Christ during the week. I am able to know who they are and rejoice with them in their newfound faith.

I will say to them, "At the end of my message this morning I am going to ask all those who have received Christ this week to leave their seats and join me for a prayer at the front, and I am going to look for you to be the first one to come! Our mutual friend Bob, here, will come with you, and you can stand together for Christ." Invariably, the individual will promise to respond at the time of invitation. It is not unusual for me to know of ten or twelve adults in one of our Sunday-morning services who, before the service begins, have already committed to make a public pledge during the invitation.

For almost fifteen years we have averaged over one thousand public decisions in our church annually, and I attribute these preservice appeals as a major factor in our success. It has a disarming effect on the ones with the deepest need to respond to the appeal. It gives them an opportunity to affirm their faith to the minister and allows them the confidence that I already am aware why they are responding to the appeal even before they come.

I continue the appeal as the service begins. Early in the worship experience we have a time to be still and acknowledge the presence of the living Lord in our midst. During this prayer time I extend the appeal by inviting the congregation to pray for those in the service who find themselves at some intersection of life with little purpose and perhaps no direction.

We thank God in advance for the many who will respond to the passionate appeal later in the service. We often pray for those on our right and our left so everyone in the building is brought before the Lord at the point of their need. I continue the appeal when we welcome our guests by making the positive affirmation that "Many of you have come thinking you are merely attending a worship service, but you are here this morning to keep a divine appointment with God Himself, and you will leave here in a few minutes with a brand-new life and a brand new beginning!" It is amazing how many can attest to how this has turned a light on in their minds, brought them to the edge of their seat in anticipation, and caused them to give serious consideration perhaps for the first time to the claims of Christ. As I continue to issue the appeal in various ways throughout the service I am seeking to build hope and expectancy in the hearts of my hearers.

The public appeal continues throughout the body of my morning message. In the introduction to the sermon I seek to provide a "hook" for the appeal and attempt to set it throughout the message. I spend considerable time in study, seeking to make a smooth transition from the sermon into the actual public appeal (see ch. 19). I have now arrived at the crucial moment when I actually appeal to my hearers to make a public response to the gospel of Jesus Christ. Everything preceding the public appeal has led up to it, and it thus becomes a sort of hinge on which the experience of corporate worship turns. By this I mean that what comes before it and what comes after it both point toward it.

The public appeal continues after the actual invitation has concluded. We receive our morning offering after the public appeal. As the people have gathered at the altar in the time of invitation I have a prayer with them and invite them to turn to the left and follow one of our members into the welcome center, as described in previous chapters.

At this time we receive our offering, and I continue the

appeal by saying to the congregation, "I know that many of you have never been in a service like this one and feel in your heart you should have responded with these others to Christ's appeal this morning. It is not a bit unusual in our church for people to continue to come even during the offering. Our ministers will be at the end of your aisle here at the front to receive you. By your coming forward during the offering you will be saying that you do not want to leave here this morning without settling this with Christ. Don't go away without Him. Come now even during the offering, take one of the ministers by the hand; they know why you are coming." The spirit of the appeal is now carried over during the playing of the offertory and every week in one or more of our multiple services, men and women respond to the appeal during the offering.

I continue the appeal as I dismiss the people. I am aware that many of my hearers are under the conviction of the Holy Spirit and are about to leave without making a conscious decision for Christ. As I dismiss the people I point them to the card in front of them in the pew rack which says, *I am interested in knowing more about spiritual things*. I encourage those with whom the Lord is dealing to take the card to our welcome center. I assure them they will find a warm welcome at the reception desk and can obtain some material to help them. We will be happy to sit down with them and lead them to faith in Christ.

Every week men and women show up in the welcome center after the conclusion of one of the services, indicating they do not want to leave until they have met the living Christ! Finally, as I dismiss the crowds from each worship service I challenge our people to be about the business of extending the personal appeal throughout the week by saying, "Someone you know needs to receive

Jesus this week. I will be looking for you and that someone by your side next Sunday!"

The public appeal should not be thought of as a single, solitary portion of the corporate worship experience. It is an attitude which must permeate the entire service. Therefore, when you stand in Christ's place to extend His appeal to men and women facing eternity . . . *make it pervasive!*

Chapter 27
Make It Preclusive

One of the most important factors to be considered by those of us who extend the appeal is to preclude certain fears and objections that weigh on the minds of our hearers. For some of us it has been too long since we have put ourselves in the place of those to whom we are seeking to appeal with the good news. We need to try to think like they do in order to preclude any unspoken barriers and preconceived ideas our hearers might feel could keep them from Christ. The best means of helping people change their minds (repent) and answer their objections is with the Word of God.

I am often aware as I extend the appeal that some of my hearers are not responding because it is all so new to them, and they are afraid of what others might think. When I am sensitive to this particular objection I may say something to the effect, "I know that some of you are wondering what others might think of you if you were to join those who have come to respond openly and publicly to Christ's call. However, I want to remind you that Jesus said, 'If anyone is ashamed of me and my words, . . . the Son of Man will be ashamed of him when he comes in his

Father's glory' (Mark 8:38). Be more concerned this morning about what Christ would think than what others will think." By using God's Word in the time of appeal I have, with great authority, broken down a barrier and built a bridge over a difficult objection making it easy for the hearers to come to Christ.

While others are in the "valley of decision" they fear that because of a previous life-style God will not accept them. As I extend the appeal I never try to preclude this objection with common sense, but always with the Word of God. I will say, "I sense that some of you are saying to yourself you are afraid to be vulnerable, and if you respond to Christ He may not accept you. Well, I have good news for you. Jesus said, 'Him that cometh to me I will in no wise cast out' (John 6:37, KJV). He will receive you just as you are and make something beautiful out of your life."

In times of appeal God's Word is our most effective weapon. To those who fail to respond to the gospel call for what they consider the inconsistency of Christians whom they have known and watched, we can appeal to them by reminding them that "[everyone must] give an account of himself to God" (Rom. 14:12). Some of our hearers may be more concerned about the fact that they are not willing to give up all to follow the Lord Jesus. They need to be reminded of this question, "What shall it profit a man if he shall gain the whole world, and lose his own soul?" (Mark 8:36, KJV). There are several of our hearers who see no real need to respond to Christ because they feel they are doing the best they can and God should accept that. This group should be reminded of the fact that the Bible says, "whosoever shall keep the whole law, and yet offend in one point, he is guilty of all" (Jas. 2:10, KJV).

For those who genuinely feel they have sinned too

much to come, we can break down their barriers with the beautiful fact that "though your sins are like scarlet, they shall be as white as snow" (Isa. 1:18). One of the most perplexing dangers in the minds of several of our hearers week by week is that they think by postponing Christ's call they will have adequate time in the future to respond. It behooves us to remind them that the Bible says, "Boast not thyself of tomorrow; for thou knowest not what a day may bring forth" (Prov. 27:1, KJV). The simple truth is there will not always be adequate time to respond in faith.

The time of public and personal appeals is when the most fierce spiritual battles are being waged. The enemy seeks to put all kinds of objections and fears in the minds of our hearers. Our only offensive weapon in this conflict is the Word of God. Use it. And, when you extend the appeal . . . *make it preclusive!*

Chapter 28
Make It Productive

In fishing for men, it is not enough to cast the net or even to draw the net, as important and mandatory as that may be. Once the net has been drawn, our task has only begun. Then we must retrieve the fish from the net and harvest them.

This involves training and discipleship of new converts so our churches do not become a mile wide and an inch deep. One of the characteristics of the first church was that their converts "devoted themselves in the apostles' teaching" (Acts 2:42). The preservation of new converts is the proof of an evangelistic appeal with truth and integrity. The lack of preservation of new converts is not only the result of poor follow-up but often the result of manipulation in the time of invitation.

In our church we offer the public appeal for two primary reasons. It gives an opportunity for those who have made a personal decision for Christ during the week to "confess [him] before men" (Matt. 10:32, KJV). Second, the public appeal provides an opportunity to present a personal appeal to those who respond as inquirers. We seek to make the appeal productive by dealing with each one who re-

sponds personally in our welcome center. This is done by
one of scores of our trained laypersons who has completed
a sixteen-week training course in evangelism which includes a minicourse in systematic theology, Scripture
memory, the articulation of our faith, and counseling
technique.

In a private room at the welcome center, spiritual birth
usually takes place with a trained counselor. Before the
new convert leaves the welcome center, he or she is introduced to one of the workers in our New Beginnings De-
partment who immediately signs them up to begin an
eight-week course on the fundamentals of our faith. Here
the new believer is given a notebook and begins the excit-
ing journey of learning to pray, to study God's Word, to
fellowship with others, and to follow the other basics of
the Christian life.

As soon as New Beginnings is completed we seek to
assimilate the new believer into a small-group Bible study
where she or he is taught to discover his or her spiritual
gifts in order to become an active participant in one of our
nearly one hundred ongoing ministries. As soon as possible we encourage our new converts to enroll in our evangelism training ministry so they can learn to articulate
their newfound faith as a way of life. Those fresh "out of
the world" know the most lost people and can have the
most significant impact on those most in need of Christ.

Public as well as personal appeals are not the end but
only the beginning of the harvest. So, as you extend
Christ's appeal be certain that you . . . *make it productive!*

Chapter 29
Make It Providential

All the modern techniques, innovations, and sharpening of skills involved in issuing a public or personal appeal can never take the place or substitute for the necessity of Divine intervention, the absolute and utter dependence on the Holy Spirit to work in and through us and others. Before we venture out to the place of witness and appeal we should make sure we "receive power" and that the Holy Spirit has come on us in order that we may become effective "witnesses" of His saving grace. The Bible promises that "You will receive power when the Holy Spirit comes on you; and you will be my witnesses in Jerusalem, and in all Judea and Samaria, and to the ends of the earth" (Acts 1:8). This is our marvelous privilege, commission, and calling.

In assessing questions arising from these words of our Lord immediately before His ascension, our spiritual forefathers, who so effectively offered personal and public appeals, captured this providential element, were filled with God's power, and fulfilled Acts 1:8 in their generation—without modern methods of technology and rapid transit. Nothing suffices for the power of the Holy Spirit in our witness. I want to repeat those words: *nothing suffices for the power of the Holy Spirit in our witness.*

The first question to be dealt with is *who?* Jesus used an imperative in the future sense when He said, "You will be my witnesses," in order to indicate that no believer was excluded or beyond Christ's commission. In extending the personal appeal there is also the question of *what?* What is it we are to receive? "Power!" This is our dire need today when many believers are anemic in their witness. We derive our English word, *dynamite,* from the Greek word (*dunamis*) translated "power" in Acts 1:8. The early church had power through the Holy Spirit. They did not have a lot of influence. They were not influential enough to keep their leaders out of prison, but they were powerful enough to pray them out! Too many of us falter and fail in our appeals because we have confused influence with power. All of the influence we may exert, along with persuasive words and winsome warmth, can never take the place of power that comes only from the Spirit of God.

In extending the appeal we must also address the question of *when?* That is, when do you receive this power to witness? You receive this power "when the Holy Spirit comes on you." When the dynamic power of the Spirit abides within us and fills us, sharing the good news and offering Christ's appeal becomes as natural as water running downhill. We will be like the early followers who could not help "speaking about what we have seen and heard" (Acts 4:20).

The appeal also brings us face to face with the question of *why?* Why does the Holy Spirit come upon us? Why do we receive power? For one reason: "[To] be my witnesses."

If you are born again you have Christ resident in you. If you have Christ, you have the Holy Spirit. If you have the

Spirit, you have power, and if you have power you are to be a witness. God does not fill us with His Spirit and power in order for us to become the judge, the prosecuting attorney, the defense, or the jury. He gives us power so we might be His "witnesses."

As we extend His appeal in public or in private we need to remember this. We are not recruiters trying to entice and induce others to join our little club. We are not salesmen trying to pressure others into buying our product. We are witnesses of Christ and His saving grace. We take the stand to testify to others from our own personal experience what we know of Him.

Yes, all of us are the recipients of power which comes only from God, the Holy Spirit, to enable us to be His witnesses, and effectively to offer His appeal to others.

In assuring we hold to the providential element of the appeal there is one other question: *where?* Where are we to take this good news and make this personal appeal? We are literally to take this appeal across the city, country, continent, and the entire cosmos. In Christ's own words we are to appeal to those in "Jerusalem, and in all Judea and Samaria, and to the ends of the earth." Those who stood with Him on the mountaintop in Jerusalem took Him at His word, and in thirty years they fulfilled His words by offering personal and public appeals as their way of life everywhere they went. Their appeals to others to follow Christ began in their own hometown. The glamour of going to a faraway place to be His witness did not supersede the importance of beginning at home. We cannot play leapfrog with the call and commission of Christ. Witnessing of Him and for Him begins in our own "Jerusalem" and extends wherever we go "to the ends of the earth."

With over five billion people on the planet, ours is an awesome task. But think about those followers of the Lord who began it all. For them it seemed *geographically impossible*. Most believed the world was flat! It seemed *physically impossible*. There were no air travel, printing presses, radios, televisions, telephones, facsimile machines, or computers with Bible study notes.

It all seemed *legally impossible*. It was against the law to speak in Christ's name in many places. And it certainly seemed *socially impossible*. By and large, the church was made up of rejects and outcasts of society. But *they did it!* They realized there was no hope in their own strength so they simply took Christ at His word. They received His power in the fullness of His Spirit, and it resulted in their becoming His witnesses. Wherever they went they extended His appeal personally and publicly, and the church mushroomed in one generation.

What is the bottom line? As you extend Christ's appeal in the public sector or in a private forum, above all else . . . *make it providential!*

Chapter 30
Make It Prudent

The issuance of Christ's appeal demands credibility, truth, and honor on the part of the one who extends it. Some pastors and evangelists have lost credibility with their congregations by not being prudent in the pulpit. There are times when, in the intensity of a public appeal, the speaker has stated to the effect, "We will sing two more stanzas of the invitation hymn, and if no one comes we will close the appeal." Two more stanzas are then sung, no one responds, and the speaker continues the appeal. At this point serious danger is done to the truth and integrity of the appeal itself.

Above all else, the public appeal demands prudence from the one called to extend it. The same is true for those of us engaged in presenting the personal and private appeal to others. Use prudence and be honest, open, and truthful in your approach. The reputation of our Lord is at stake as you witness of Him and offer His appeal.

Honesty in Christ's appeal means we have adequately presented the gospel before we offer it to others. I believe we should always give some type of evangelistic appeal after the gospel is presented, but I believe the reverse is also true. The gospel should always be presented *before* an appeal is offered. We have all heard of evangelists who tell one deathbed story after another, moving on the emotions of the hearers. Yet they never zero in on the good news, the fact that "God made him who had no sin to be sin for us, so that in him we might become the righteousness of God" (2 Cor. 5:21). Strictly emotional appeals, devoid of the heart of the gospel, are the reason for much fallout of many "new converts."

There is certainly nothing wrong with the emotional element in the appeal. I'm sure Moses became a little emotional when the bush continued to burn, and he heard God's voice from it! What is wrong and dishonest is for us to offer an appeal to others that is devoid of the heart of the gospel and is not clear about the demands of discipleship.

Be truthful in your appeals to others. Do not give people a false hope. Your hearers will forgive you for almost anything. However, they have a hard time forgiving you for dishonesty, manipulation, and trickery, especially when you stand as Christ's representative to a lost world desperately in need of purpose and peace that only He can give. As you extend the appeal publicly or personally make sure you . . . *make it prudent!*

Appendix A
The Public Appeal

(The following is a word-by-word example of the public appeal as it is extended Sunday after Sunday in the First Baptist Church of Fort Lauderdale, Florida. The author's primary intent is to use the public appeal to give opportunity for those in attendance who have recently received the free gift of eternal life to make a public pledge of such by "confessing Christ before men." And it is used to encourage inquirers to respond in such a fashion that they can be dealt with individually by a trained counselor in the "welcome center" immediately following the public appeal. The scene for the public appeal is set as the message is concluded and the transition to the appeal is made. The congregation remains seated with bowed heads, and the pastor initiates the appeal as follows.)

"In just a moment I am going to ask you to do something that is going to take courage. I am going to ask you to leave your seat, step into the aisle, make your way to the front, and join me here for a prayer. Many of you are going to come to be included in this prayer this morning. Some of you have never opened your heart's door to receive the free gift of eternal life, Jesus Christ, as your very own personal Savior. You have a Divine appointment with Him this morning, and you are not here by accident.

"Perhaps you sense God's Spirit knocking at the door of your heart but, quite honestly, just don't know what you would say if you were to respond and join me here at the front. I have good news for you. You do not have to worry about what to say. By your coming you will be saying, 'I am going to go God's way today!' When you get here, I am going to lead us all in a word of prayer. We have some Bible study material to give you to help you, and if you come as an inquirer we want the privilege of leading you to faith in the Lord Jesus. By trusting in Him alone this morning it will mean God will forgive you of all your sin and make it just as if it never happened. It also means that Christ, Himself, will take up residence in your life and never leave you. It means He will give you a place in heaven and a heavenly time on the way. So, in just a moment, I am going to ask you to come and receive this free gift.

"There are others of you here this morning who have already opened your hearts to Christ; perhaps this week, last week, last month, or whenever. But you have never stood for Him publicly, openly, or unashamedly. In just a moment, I am going to ask you to join the others who are coming, and, by your coming to be included in this prayer, you will be saying, 'I am making a public pledge of my life to Jesus Christ.'

"There is something about it that will help seal it in your life. Our Lord never called anyone to follow Him that He did not do so publicly. At the seaside He called the fishermen to follow Him in front of all their business associates and friends. In Jericho He called Zacchaeus to follow Him in front of the huge crowd lining the street.

There is just something about standing for Christ publicly that helps seal the personal decision that has already been made in the heart. In fact, Jesus said, 'Whosoever therefore shall confess me before men, him will I confess also before my Father which is in heaven' (Matt. 10:32, KJV). How can you expect to stand for Christ in the market-places of the world, which are so hostile to Him, if you will not stand for him by walking down a carpeted aisle of an air-conditioned church in front of a lot of Christians who will rejoice with you in your decision? Therefore, in a moment when others come I am going to ask you to lead the way to this altar.

"Still others of you are here who are Christians but not active in a local church in our city. Perhaps you have just moved here. You have moved everything you have—your furniture, your family, even your pets. Everything, that is, except your church membership. In a moment, I am going to ask you to join the others in coming and by doing so you will be saying, 'I am going to come out of the shadows today and put on the uniform of church membership and serve Christ in and through this local expression of His body.' You have been eating your spiritual food here for some time. You have been thinking about joining our team. You have even been planning on it and praying about it. The only thing left is to do it right now. By your coming to join us this morning and being included in this prayer you will also be serving as an escort for many here who need to know Jesus Christ personally.

"There are yet others of you here this morning with a friend who needs to know Jesus. It may be that the Spirit of God would have you reach out and take that friend by the hand and say, 'Let's go God's way this morning. I'll go with you. Let's go together!' Many in the Bible did that very thing. Andrew found Peter, took him by the hand, and brought him to Jesus. Philip brought Nathaniel. And on and on the church has grown. You can be confident that if the Spirit is leading you to encourage your friend He is dealing with his heart at the same time. When He leads a Philip to the Gaza desert it is because He is working on the heart of an Ethiopian and wants him to take him by the hand and bring him to Jesus. When He leads a Peter to Caesarea it is because He is simultaneously working on the heart of a Cornelius. Take your friend by the hand this morning and say, 'Let's go together. I'll go with you.' And bring your friend to Jesus. You will be so glad you did.

"There are others of you who are here this morning and honest enough to say, 'Preacher, I don't know what I need. But my life has no purpose, or peace, or direction.' The something you have looked for to fill the void of life can be found this morning in Someone, and His sweet name is the Lord Jesus. I am going to ask you to join the others in coming to be included in this prayer. Don't worry about what to say when you get here. By your coming as an inquirer you will be saying, 'I want to go God's way today and trust in Him.' And when you come, 'Your sins He'll wash away, your night He'll turn to day, your life . . . He'll make it over anew.' He has a brand-new life for you and a brand-new beginning!

"Whatever the decision may be in your heart—a desire to know Christ personally, a public pledge of your life to Him, to unite with our fellowship and join our 'team,' to bring a friend to Jesus, or simply to come in honest inquiry, I am going to ask you to leave your seat, make your way to the front, and join me here. By your coming you are saying, 'I am going God's way today.' Don't wait for anyone else. If there is the slightest tugging at your heartstrings it is the Spirit of God. Many are going to come, and it is the right thing to do. You lead the way right now!"

(At this point in the public appeal the congregation remains seated in a spirit of prayer while men and women, boys and girls respond to the appeal. There are times when, as the Spirit directs, the appeal is extended most generally in one of the following ways using the Word of God.)

"The Bible says, 'Today, *if* you hear his voice, do not harden your hearts' (Heb. 3:8,15; 4:7, author's italics). I am speaking finally and fleetingly to those of you who are here who 'hear his voice' in your heart. You will know it if you do. It is as if He is knocking at your heart's door and pulling at your heartstrings. Every time He calls and you refuse, your heart gets a little harder. In fact, the word the Bible uses to describe this is 'callous' (Eph. 4:19). If you have had a callous you are aware you can stick a pin in it and never feel it. Continually refusing Christ's call has the same effect on your heart. There may come a time when, even though He is still calling, you no longer will hear. That is why there is an urgency in this hour. If there is the slightest feeling in your heart that God is calling you to Himself, come now. Yes, '*today*, if you hear his voice, do not harden your hearts' (author's italics).

"The Bible says, 'Seek the Lord while he may be found; call on him while he is near' (Isa. 55:6). He is waiting for you this morning. He is very near your heart. Yes, Jesus is passing by your heart this very moment. Some of you are closer to coming to Him than you have been in a lifetime. You may never be this close again. Seize the moment. He will meet you like the father met his prodigal son, with open arms, no pointed fingers, or clenched fists, just wide-open arms which say, 'Come.'

"The Bible says, 'The Spirit himself testifies with our spirit that we are God's children' (Rom. 8:16). Perhaps you are uncertain of your eternal destiny. Bow your head and ask yourself the question, *Am I saved?* Does the Holy Spirit bear witness with your spirit? The Bible also says, 'Those who are led by the Spirit of God are sons of God' (v. 14). What is the Holy Spirit leading you to do this morning? Think about it.

"If you are here without Christ what do you think He is leading you to do? He will not lead you to walk out those back doors in rejection or neglect. If you have placed your trust in Him but never let anyone know it, what do you suppose He is leading you to do right now? Walk out and continue being a secret disciple? Or join us at this altar in an open pledge of your life to Him who stood for you in life through death and to life again?

"If you are here and are not active in a local church what do you suppose He is leading you to do? When you are in the United States Army you are not just a part of a world-wide endeavor. You are assigned to a local base where you are accountable and are given assignments of service. The same holds true in God's army. He assigns us to local bases, and perhaps He is assigning you here today.

"If you are with a friend who needs to know Jesus, what do you suppose Jesus is leading you to do? Encourage your friend toward Christ or walk out without a word?

Yes, 'Those are led by the Spirit of God are sons of God.' God, the Holy Spirit, is leading you this morning to the Lord Jesus Christ and by your coming to join these many others already here, you will be indicating you are going God's way today. And, it is the right thing to do. I will meet you as you come."

Appendix B
The Personal Appeal

The church's public appeal stands upon the effectiveness of its individual member's personal appeals for Christ in the normal traffic patterns of life. A great number of those who respond to the public appeals in the First Baptist Church of Fort Lauderdale do so because they have been personally led to faith in Christ by laypersons who have been trained to share their faith as a life-style. Since 1978 the church has trained thousands of its members in Evangelism Explosion, many of whom have scattered all over America and the world encouraging others to become active in personal evangelism. There are many good evangelism training courses available today. Many of our own Southern Baptist churches are involved with Continued Witness Training. The following personal appeals are the planned programs of personal appeal used to train the author's army of lay evangelists at First Baptist Church in Fort Lauderdale.

Do You Know for Sure
You Are Going to Heaven?

If God were to ask you "WHY SHOULD I LET YOU INTO MY HEAVEN?" what would you say? If you are uncertain or hesitate for a moment to answer that question, this booklet has the . . . best news you could ever hear! The few minutes it will take you to read the following pages may be the most important time you will ever spend! Did you know that the Bible tells how you can KNOW FOR SURE that you have eternal life and will go to be with God in heaven?

These things I have written to you . . . that you may know that you have eternal life (1 John 5:13).

Here's how you can KNOW FOR SURE . . .

1. HEAVEN (ETERNAL LIFE) IS A FREE GIFT.

The Bible says, "the GIFT of God is *eternal life in Christ Jesus our Lord"* (Romans 6:23b). And because heaven is a gift like any other genuine gift . . . IT IS NOT EARNED OR DESERVED. Therefore, no amount of personal effort, good works, or religious deeds can earn a place in heaven for you.

By grace you have been saved through faith; and NOT OF YOUR-SELVES; it is the gift of God, NOT OF WORKS, lest any man should boast (Ephesians 2:8,9) WHY is it that no one can earn his way to heaven?

Because . . .

2. MAN IS A SINNER.

All have sinned and fall short of the glory of God (Romans 3:23). Sin is transgressing God's law and includes such things as lust, cheating, deceit, anger, evil thoughts, immoral behavior, and more.

And because of this . . .

MAN CANNOT SAVE HIMSELF.

If you wanted to save yourself by good deeds, do you know how good you would have to be?

The Bible says you would have to be *perfect.*

Therefore you shall be perfect, just as your Father in heaven is perfect (Matthew 5:48).

With such a high standard, no one can save himself for God also says,

Whoever shall keep the whole law, and yet stumble in one point, he is guilty of all (James 2:10).

In spite of our sin, however...

3. GOD IS MERCIFUL, and therefore DOESN'T WANT TO PUNISH US.
This is because...

"God is love..." (1 John 4:8b).
and He says,
"I have loved you with an everlasting love" (Jeremiah 31:3b).

But the same Bible that tells us that God loves us also tells us that...

GOD IS JUST, and therefore MUST PUNISH SIN.
He says...
"I will by no means clear the guilty..." (Exodus 34:7b).
"The soul who sins shall die (Ezekiel 18:4).

We have a problem; we have all sinned. The penalty for sin is death. We need forgiveness so that we can have a right relationship with God.

God solved this problem for us in the Person of...

4. JESUS CHRIST
Who exactly would you say Jesus Christ is?
The Bible tells us clearly that He is the infinite GOD-MAN.

In the beginning was the Word (Jesus) . . . and the Word (Jesus) was with God . . . and the Word (Jesus) became flesh and dwelt among us . . . (John 1:1,14).

Jesus Christ came to earth and lived a sinless life, but while on earth . . .

WHAT DID HE DO?

He died on the cross to pay the penalty for our sins and rose from the grave to purchase a place for us in heaven.

All we like sheep have gone astray; we have turned every one to his own way; and the Lord has laid on Him the iniquity of us all (Isaiah 53:6).

God hates our sins but because of His love for us, He has placed them all on His Son. Christ bore our sin in His body on the cross.

Now Jesus Christ offers you eternal life (heaven) as a free gift. **This gift is received by . . .**

5. FAITH

Faith is the key that opens the door to heaven. Many people mistake two things for saving faith:

1. Mere INTELLECTUAL ASSENT, that is, believing certain historical facts. The Bible says the devil believes in God, so believing in God is not saving faith.

2. Mere TEMPORAL FAITH, that is, trusting God for temporary crises such as financial, family, or physical needs. Now these are good, and you should trust Christ for these, but they are not saving faith!

SAVING FAITH is trusting in Jesus Christ alone for salvation. It means resting upon Christ alone and what He has done rather than upon what you or I have done to get us into heaven.

Believe (trust) on the Lord Jesus Christ, and you will be saved . . . (Acts 16:31a).

Faith is like the hand of a beggar receiving the gift of a King. We don't deserve the gift of eternal life. But we can have it, if we will receive it by faith.

You have just read the greatest story ever told about the greatest offer ever made by the greatest Person who ever lived— Jesus Christ. The question that God is asking you now is . . .

WOULD YOU LIKE TO RECEIVE THE GIFT OF ETERNAL LIFE?

Because this is such an important matter. . . **LET'S CLARIFY** just what this involves. It means, first of all, that you TRANSFER YOUR TRUST from what you have been doing to what Christ has done for you on the cross. It means, next, that you RECEIVE THE RESURRECTED, LIVING CHRIST into your life as SAVIOR. He says, *Behold, I stand at the door and knock (at the door of your life). If any one hears My voice and opens the door, I will come in to him* (Revelation 3:20).

It means further that you RECEIVE JESUS CHRIST INTO YOUR LIFE AS LORD. He comes as Master and King. There is a throne room in your heart, and that throne is rightly His. He made you. He bought you and He wants to take His rightful place on the throne of your life. It means, finally, that you REPENT OF YOUR SINS. That means that you are willing to turn from anything you have been doing that is not pleasing to Him and to follow Him as He reveals His will to you in His Word.

Now, if this is what you really want . . .

YOU CAN GO TO GOD IN PRAYER right where you are. You can receive His gift of eternal life through Jesus Christ right now. . . . *With the heart one believes to righteousness and with the mouth confession is made to salvation . . . for whoever calls upon the name of the Lord shall be saved* (Romans 10:10,13). If you want to receive the gift of eternal life through Jesus Christ, then call on Him, asking Him for this gift right now.

HERE'S A SUGGESTED PRAYER: "Lord Jesus Christ, I know I am a sinner and do not deserve eternal life. But, I believe you died and rose from the grave to purchase a place in heaven for me. Lord Jesus, come into my life; take control of my life; forgive my sins and save me. I repent of my sins and now place my trust in you for my salvation. I accept the free gift of eternal life." If this prayer is the sincere desire of your heart, look at what Jesus promises to those who believe in Him.

Most assuredly, I say to you, he who believes in Me has everlasting life (John 6:47).

WELCOME to God's Family!

If you have truly repented (forsaken, turned away) from your sins, placed your trust in Jesus Christ's sacrificial death, and received the gift of eternal life, you are now a child of God! Forever! Welcome to the Family of God!

But as many as received Him, to them He gave the right to become children of God, even to those who believe in His name (John 1:12).

TODAY is your SPIRITUAL BIRTHDAY—

a day that you will always want to remember! *Who were born, not of blood, nor of the will of the flesh, nor of the will of man, but of God* (John 1:13).

When you were physically born, the day of your birth was attested by a birth certificate.

And so today, to help you recall what God has done in your life on this important day, we invite you to sign and keep the following . . .

SPIRITUAL BIRTH CERTIFICATE

For whosoever calls upon the name of the Lord shall be saved (Romans 10:13). Knowing that I have sinned and that I need the Lord Jesus Christ as my Savior, I now turn from my sins and trust Jesus for my eternal life. I ask Jesus Christ to forgive me and to deliver me from sin's power and give me eternal life.

I now give Jesus Christ control of my life.

From this time forward, as He gives me strength, I will seek to serve Him and obey Him in all areas of my life.

Date _____

Signature: _____

WHAT'S NEXT? Just as a newborn baby grows physically, so you will grow spiritually by taking the following steps:

1. Read one chapter of the Book of John in the **BIBLE** each day.

As newborn babes, desire the pure milk of the Word (of God), that you may grow thereby (1 Peter 2:2).

2. Spend time each day in **PRAYER** conversing with God. *Be anxious for nothing, but in everything by prayer and supplication, with thanksgiving, let your requests be made known to God . . .* (Philippians 4:6).

3. **WORSHIP** regularly in a church that teaches you the Bible and honors Jesus Christ.

I was glad when they said to me, "Let us go into the house of the Lord" (Psalm 122:1).

God is Spirit, and those who worship Him must worship in spirit and truth (John 4:24).

4. **FELLOWSHIP** with Christians who will help you grow in faith.

Those who gladly received His word . . . continued steadfastly in the apostles' doctrine and fellowship, in the breaking of bread, and in prayers (Acts 2:41,42).

5. Be a **WITNESS** by telling others what Jesus Christ means to you!

Jesus said, *Therefore whoever confesses Me before men, him I will also confess before my Father who is in heaven. But whoever denies me before men, him I will also deny before My Father who is in heaven* (Matthew 10:32,33).

Remember to attend regularly a Bible-teaching **CHURCH** where

Jesus Christ is honored. Confess your faith in Christ to them and join it.

Not forsaking the assembling of ourselves together, as is the manner of some . . . (Hebrews 10:25).

(Used by permission of Evangelism Explosion III, International, P. O. Box 23820, Fort Lauderdale, Florida.)

★ ★ ★

The following personal appeal was developed by the Evangelism Division of the Home Mission Board of the Southern Baptist Convention and is effectively used in churches across the nation.

Do You Know for Certain That You Have Eternal Life and That You Will Go to Heaven When You Die?

God wants you to be sure.
The Bible says, "These things have I written unto you that believe on the name of the Son of God; that ye may know that ye have eternal life" (1 John 5:13).

Another question to consider is:
Suppose you were standing before God right now and He asked you, "Why should I let you into My heaven?" What do you think you would say?

You may not know what you would say. But . . .

You can know, because God loves us and has a purpose for our lives. The Bible states it this way, "For God so loved the world, that he gave his only begotten Son, that whosoever believeth in him should not perish, but have everlasting life" (John 3:16).

GOD'S PURPOSE
IS THAT WE HAVE ETERNAL LIFE

*We receive eternal life as a free gift.

"The gift of God is eternal life through Jesus Christ our Lord" (Rom. 6:23).

*We can live a full and meaningful life right now. "I am come that they might have life, and that they might have it more abundantly" (John 10:10).

*We will spend eternity with Jesus in heaven.

"And if I go and prepare a place for you, I will come again, and receive you to myself; that where I am, there ye may be also" (John 14:3).

Eternal life gives real meaning to life.

Yet...
Our sinful nature keeps us from fulfilling God's purpose for our lives. Thus...

OUR NEED IS TO UNDERSTAND OUR PROBLEM.

*We are all sinners by nature and by choice.

"For all have sinned, and come short of the glory of God" (Rom. 3:23).

*We cannot save ourselves.

"Not of works, lest any man should boast" (Eph. 2:9).

*We deserve death and hell.

"For the wages of sin is death" (Rom. 6:23).

It is true that:

God is holy and just and must punish sin, yet He loves us and has provided forgiveness for our sin. Jesus said, "I am the way, the truth, and the life; no man cometh unto the Father, but by me" (John 14:6).

The Good News is that God has provided for the forgiveness of our sins.

GOD'S PROVISION IS JESUS CHRIST.

*Jesus is God and became man.
"In the beginning was the Word, and the Word was with God, and the Word was God. . . . And the Word became flesh, and dwelt among us" (John 11:1,14).

*Jesus died for us on the cross.
"For Christ also hath once suffered for sins, the just for the unjust, that he might bring us to God" (1 Pet. 3:18).

*Jesus was resurrected from the dead.
"(Jesus) was delivered for our offences, and was raised again for our justification" (Rom. 4:25).

That is good news, . . . but the only way Jesus can affect our lives is for us to receive him. The Bible says, "But as many as received him, to them he gave the power to become the sons of God, even to them that believe on his name" (John 1:12).

The choice is ours. Thus . . .

OUR RESPONSE IS TO RECEIVE JESUS.

*We must repent of our sin. "Repent ye therefore, and be converted, that your sins may be blotted out" (Acts 3:19).

Repentance is not just feeling sorry for our sin. "Repent and turn to God, and do works meet for (which give evidence of) repentance" (Acts 26:20).

Repentance is turning away from our sin and turning to God through Jesus. It's like making a U-turn.

As we turn . . .

*We must place our faith in Jesus.
"For by grace are we saved through faith; and that not of yourselves: it is the gift of God" (Eph. 2:8).

Faith is not just believing facts about Jesus. "Thou believest that there is one God; thou doest well: the devils also believe, and tremble" (James 2:19).

Faith is trusting in Jesus. It's like taking a trip on an airplane. You will never make the trip until you trust the plane enough to board it.

To trust totally in Jesus, means . . .

We must surrender to Jesus as Lord.
"That if thou shalt confess with thy mouth the Lord Jesus, and shalt believe in thine heart that God hath raised him from the dead, thou shalt be saved. For. . . with the mouth confession is made unto salvation" (Rom. 10:9-10).

Surrendering to Jesus as Lord is not just saying we give our lives to Jesus. "Not every one that saith unto me, Lord, Lord, shall enter into the kingdom of heaven; but he that doeth the will of my Father, which is in heaven" (Matt. 7:21).

Surrendering to Jesus as Lord is giving Jesus control of our lives.

To give Jesus control of our lives is like driving down the highway with another person. As long as you are driving, you are in control. If, at some point, you realize you don't know the way, but the other person does, and you say, "You take the wheel and drive," then the other person is in control and the two of you take the route he chooses.

As *evidence* of giving Jesus control, you will want to *identify* with him. The New Testament way is to confess Jesus publicly (Matt. 10:32-33) and to follow him in baptism and church membership (Acts 2:41).

THREE IMPORTANT QUESTIONS:

*Does what you have been reading make sense to you?

*Is there any reason why you would not be willing to receive God's gift of eternal life?

*Are you willing to turn from your sin and place your faith in Jesus right now?

The Bible says, "For whosoever shall call upon the name of the Lord shall be saved" (Rom. 10:13).

You need to ask the Lord to save you.

Please read this prayer and see if it is what you want to say to God.
   Dear Lord, I believe you are the Son of God, and that you died on the cross and were raised from the dead. I know I have sinned and need forgiveness. I turn from my sins and receive you as my Savior and Lord. Thank you for saving me.

Call upon the Lord in repentance, faith and surrender, using these or similar words of your own; and Jesus will become your Savior and Lord. Thank you for saving me.

Welcome to the family of God. You have just made the most important decision of your life. You can be sure you are saved and have eternal life because . . .

Call upon the Lord in repentance, faith and surrender, using these or similar words of your own: and Jesus will become your Savior and Lord.

YOUR ASSURANCE . . . You can know you have eternal life because:
God keeps His promises.

   *You repented of your sin (Acts 3:19).
   *You placed your faith in Jesus (Eph. 2:8-9).
   *You surrendered to Jesus as Lord (Rom. 10:9-10).

God heard your prayer.
   "Whosoever shall call upon the name of the Lord shall be saved" (Rom. 10:13).

God recorded your commitment.

". . . rejoice, because your names are written in heaven" (Luke 10:20).

You need to grow as a Christian.

The Bible calls new Christians "babes in Christ" (1 Cor. 3:1). Without certain essentials, babies will not develop normally.

The church is to a new Christian what the *home and family* are to a new baby.

You identify with your new family by confessing Jesus publicly; and by experiencing believer's baptism. "Then they that gladly received the word were baptized: and the same day there were added unto them about three thousand souls" (Acts 2:41).

Attend church Sunday and share with the pastor that you desire to be baptized and become a member of the church.

Praying is to a new Christian what breathing is to a new baby. Breathing must be regular and continuous. The Bible says, "Pray without ceasing" (1 Thess. 5:17).

Learn to be specific in your praying. "If we confess our sins, he is faithful and just to forgive us our sins, and to cleanse us from all unrighteousness" (1 John 1:9).

God's Word is to a new Christian what *good food* is to a new baby.

Good food is a daily requirement for proper growth. "As newborn babes, desire the sincere milk of the word, that you may grow thereby" (1 Pet. 2:2).

My best time to pray and read the Bible each day is _____.

Learning to witness is to a new Christian what *learning to talk* is to a new baby. Christ commands us to share the good news with others. "And ye shall be witnesses" (Acts 1:8).

Write the name of a person who will be happy to learn about your decision for Christ _____,
and the name of a person who needs to receive Christ _____
_____.

Be sure to tell them about your new life as soon as possible.

I received Christ _____

(Date)

_____

(Name)

(Used by permission of the Home Mission Board of the Southern Baptist Convention.)